# The CALLING
# of the
# CHILDREN of the LIGHT

RICK HATALA

and

SHANNON SAMBELLS

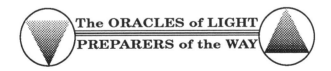

The ORACLES of LIGHT
PREPARERS of the WAY

ISBN: 1-895794-00-5

PREPARERS of the WAY
P.O.Box 22204 - Bankers Hall
Calgary, Alberta, CANADA
T2P-4J5

First Edition ..................... March, 1992
Second Edition ............. September, 1992

Illustrated and Designed by Rick Hatala
Page layout and design by Mary Winters

Printed in Canada

## DEDICATION

We dedicate this book to our
Soul and Earthly families

Nancy, Jennie, Andrew

Harry, Gaela, Richard, Chelsea

# ACKNOWLEDGEMENTS

We would like to acknowledge all the Great Teachers, Sages, and Mystics who have prepared the way for this time.

We would further like to acknowledge the guidance, direction, and insights given by the Oracles of Light during the writing of this book. The angelic realm has worked to clarify concepts and to move our finite thinking into closer alignment with Divine principles.

We have not only felt the power of their realm, but their love for all mankind. We feel blessed in being given the opportunity to participate in this work.

# An OUTLINE of the MESSAGE

# An OUTLINE of the MESSAGE

**THIRD PORTION:     IMPACTING OUR
                     RELATIONSHIPS**

**FOURTH PORTION:  The CALL to a NEW
                   APPLICATION of the ONE TRUTH**

**THE CONTINUUM - Stories on the Path**

**ABOUT THE AUTHORS**

# LIST of IMAGES

# The BLENDING of our REALITIES

Dear Children of the Light:

You are a child of the Divine and have incarnated onto the earthly-framework at this time with a special purpose and for a special mission. You may not be fully aware of who you truly are or what your special role might be, but you will have experienced a haunting to uncover the meaning of life and may have already begun to redefine your principles and beliefs.

As you begin, in earnest, to search for answers to your growing questions, you need to be aware of the changes which will occur within and outside of you, for these changes are all aspects of the "call" to remember your Divine heritage.

You may seek for insight and understanding from religious institutions, books, interest groups, friends, and a variety of different paths and programs. However, remember in all your searchings that the best source of all is your soul! Your soul carries Divine remembrance which can interact with your conscious mind and allow you to access Divine truths and universal principles. Your soul, if allowed its rightful place in your life, can lead you to illumination, cleansing, interaction with others, and ultimately, to peace, harmony, joy, and love.

In this time of transition, each of you will need to prepare for the impending turbulence and the earthly changes that have been prophecized by sages, mystics, and spiritual philosophers for eons.

As our world spins ever faster and as you rush to meet the ever growing demands that are placed upon you, you may question why your earthly life is fraught with so many complications, emotional difficulties, financial uncertainties, and seeming spiritual imbalances. These challenges are not simply random obstacles placed in your path throughout life, but are wonderfully orchestrated learnings. They are learnings which your soul, in its wisdom, guides you to experience so that you may have an opportunity to awaken to who you truly are and why you have chosen this time to be on the earth.

This is the time of the awakening to your soul. It is a time of remembrance of where you come from. It is a time of recognition of your innate talents and gifts which may have lain dormant within you. It is a time during which you may seek out others of like-mind and beliefs and purposes. It is a time during which you will be drawn into greater service to humanity.

We have found the children of the light in all walks of life, in all cultures, races, religions, vocations, and economic states. Some of these children have prepared themselves to hear and respond to the Divine call which is now resonating within their hearts and minds. Others may experience a haunting that there is something, some role, some purpose that they must strive to know and seek to fulfill.

This book was written for all souls who have heard, felt, or responded to the calling that has and continues to emanate from the heavens.

In writing the CALLING of the CHILDREN of the LIGHT, we have attempted to blend the path of man's evolving historical, mental and spiritual development with our understanding of the Divine plan for this earthly planet. We have examined the cycles of learning of the soul of mankind and have striven to integrate them into a wholistic and cohesive spiritual-framework.

What has emerged for us through the writing, and hopefully will emerge for you through your reading, is a deeper understanding of the present times in which we all live and the struggle and duality of the search for truth without (as in science and technology) and the search for truth within (as in man's personal experience of spirituality).

The writing of this book would have been impossible without assistance from the etheric and spiritual realms. The principle source of Divine inspiration came from the group of light beings known as the Oracles of Light.

The Oracles exist in the angelic dimensions and, as messengers of the Divine, desired only to help clarify the intent and the unfolding of the Divine plan in the midst of these troubled times on the earth. The Oracles have maintained a watchful eye over the progress and mani-festation of this work from the very beginning. They have helped with specific information, constructive criticism, and guidance throughout.

As the inspirational writing and editing and re-editing progressed, we began to sense a rhythm in the way the words flowed onto the page. This "rhythm" became our sign of what we came to know as the presence of the Divine and the words joined together more like poetry or prose rather than an essay. In an effort to preserve the "rhythm" or "heartbeat" of the work, we often suspended and broke many of the rules of good grammar and composition.

The emerging "rhythm" became our standard and, in a sense, inspired us to work harder and search further for greater clarity in writing, contemplating, transcribing, and interpreting these heavenly transmissions and blending them with our own knowledge and personal experiences.

This book, then, is a blended work. It is a balance between the intuitive and inspired with the rational and conscious. It is a blending of our spiritual guidance within our personal earthly experiences.

In our life journeys we have found that no one religion, philosophy, or viewpoint possesses all of the truth. However, each religion or philosophy we examined contains a portion of it. When we extracted these portions, explored, and compared them, we felt they yielded a greater and fuller understanding of God's plan for mankind on the earth.

In reading the words and reflecting on the ideas in the book, we hope that you will allow yourself to move beyond rigid religious or institutional dogma and allow the rhythm and the spirit behind this work to strike a chord within your soul. If it strikes a discord, we'd suggest you put it down and leave it until you feel you are more ready to digest and assimilate the ideas it contains.

There is a story which we both felt needed to be told. It is a glorious story for it chronicles the creation, evolution, and ascent of the soul of man. We have attempted to tell the story with clarity and simplicity in an effort to help prepare you for this time of transition and for the Golden Age of Peace that follows it.

To enable a simplicity of expression, we've chosen to use the generic form "mankind" rather than "humankind", and the generic "man" rather than wo/man or s/he which is so popular today. There is no wish to offend, for we know that the soul knows no gender or sex and that in the spirit state, we are all androgynous.

This work is only one component of the spiritual outreach that is now occurring on the earth. We hope it will convey to each of you a message of hope and a greater understanding of these times of great changes in which we all live.

We both feel very blessed for the opportunity to be instruments for this facet of the greater work of the Divine.

In seeking to understand your connection with the Divine, in desiring to know the power and the beauty which is within your own soul, in yearning to return to a state of truth and illumination, you are indeed a child of the light.

The calling of the Divine is within. The calling is occurring now. Each must choose how to respond to that call.

In Peace and in Love,

SHANNON SAMBELLS and
RICK HATALA

March, 1992
Calgary, Alberta

## The CALLING of the CHILDREN of the LIGHT

Throughout the ages, the philosophies and great teachers of mankind have heralded the dawning of the age of peace and the Golden age of mankind. As we move to the end of this millennium, there is the fulfillment of these prophecies and the transition of man's consciousness to unconditional and unremittant love.

Those who prepare for this new age and those who come to aid in this time are called the children of the light.

We come to call the Children of the Light.

This is the time of the unfolding that was prophecized. Be ready for the changes which will manifest on the earth. Be ready for the great movements around the globe and within the hearts of men.

We come to call the Children of the Light.

There will be economic fluctuations which immobilize economies, but which will serve to move mankind to one standard, one basis for trade, and one world currency.

Be prepared for the shifting and tumbling of world orders, political parties, and changes in world leadership. For remember, the world spiritual leader will show himself at the end of these troubled times!

We come to call the Children of the Light.

Ready yourselves for the changes within your hearts and minds so that you may identify truth when you learn it, hope when you see it, love when you feel it, and harmony when you live it.

We come to call the Children of the Light.

Do not be fearful, but rather be stout of heart and courageous in your vision and resulting actions. Trust in the oneness Divine. Call to your soul neighbor, even as you would call to yourself. Call to our heavenly spheres and We will aid from this dimension.

We come to call the Children of the Light.

We are the Oracles of Light and are
the Messengers of the Divine.

*Oracles of Light Reading November, 1991*

# The CALL to SPIRITUAL and GLOBAL TRANSFORMATION

## 1.1 The WAVE of TRANSITION

There is a phenomenon which is occurring on the face of the earth. It is a CHANGE. A change that will bring with it much transition and much opportunity for growth that has not been witnessed on the earth for thousands upon thousands of years.

This phenomenon is a CALLING to many souls to awaken and begin to aid in this time of transition; To begin living the covenant that lies sleeping within them; To claim the gifts of the spirit that living this covenant would give them; To help their brother and sister souls to align and attune with the DIVINE in this tumultuous time of testing.

This wave of heralded change is now manifesting. It is washing onto the shores of our earthly awareness and can be seen by those who have eyes to see.

These changes have come - not to bring into your lives only turmoil, or strife, or suffering - but to cause each to reflect and question the nature of earthly existence and to give an opportunity to view yourselves and your relationship to the Divine in a different way.

These changes will allow you to reflect on your principles. They will allow you to re-examine your beliefs and to reconsider your thoughts, feelings, and actions towards yourself and your fellow man. They will allow you to gain a new perspective on the positions you held to and clung to so firmly, by plunging you into the waters of your own emotional storms, to ride and be swept along by the wave of transition towards a new concept of self.

All souls are His children. All souls may partake of the heritage of the Divine. All souls may become aware that they are sons and daughters of the Most High. All are loved and beloved in the heavens. And in this time, all are being called into service.

For the time in which mankind lives is the time of transition from the dark age of materiality to the light age of spirituality.

It is the dawning of a new consciousness in the experience of mankind. From this illumination of consciousness a new awareness will arise. And from this new awareness, through each who responds and allows himself to be instruments of the Divine, the earth will be cleansed and regenerated.

The wave of transition is inevitable. It cannot be stopped for the seeds of this change have been planted in the distant past. The harvest of the seed-thoughts, feelings, and actions planted in the earthly consciousness are being reaped by mankind in this day.

All are being called into service and need to awaken to the spirit that underlies this wave of transition. By working in harmony with this spiritual intent, you may bring clarity, understanding, illumination, and purpose into your life and into the lives of those around you. But by working for your own purposes, you may bring chaos, darkness, and confusion into your earthly experience and into the experience of others.

This wave of transition is a time of testing. This is the time of choosing whom and what will you serve? In whom and and in what will you believe? Where have you placed your faith? In the works of God or the works of man? In the kingdom of heaven or in the kingdom of the earth? In bearing witness to the light or in the darkness? Will you bring life into the experience of yourself and others, or will you choose to bring death?

Choose. Choose what is your image of God. Is it a God of selfishness or a God of selflessness?

All are children of the Most High and each has a special purpose in this time of transition. Each has a special role to play in this earthly drama that no other soul can perform quite as well.

Just as in the earthly body of man there are cells that yield flesh, bones, blood, and tissues of every nature, each with a purpose, each with a role to perform in nurturing and sustaining the life force in the earthy-man, so is it in the consciousness of the body of mankind.

In the body of mankind, there are those souls who would help to form the fabric, the skin, and the structures of man. There are those souls who would help to minister to the sick and the ailing in body, mind, and spirit. There are those souls who would help to eliminate and cleanse the planet of waste and corruption. And there are those souls who would feed and nurture and help to sustain his collective existence on this planet.

But in this time, there are few who have prepared themselves sufficiently to hear this call of the spirit. For know that the call comes first to the spirit in man, then to his mind, then to the circumstances and situations in which he lives his earthly life.

The call - in its very essence - is the name of the Divine. And within that vibration, within that chord there is a tone that serves to awaken those souls who have descended into planet earth for a special purpose.

These children of the light are those who have come at this time in the joy of service to the Creator and to the earth. They have heard the call and have chosen to respond. They are awakening to their purpose and to their mission to help to prepare the way for the entrance of Divine consciousness to blend with earthly consciousness and to aid their brother and sister souls in this time of turmoil, tribulation, and earthly suffering.

These children have felt the call as a haunting. They believe that they are called to a work that is beyond earthly living alone, but are unfirm in their beliefs and convictions. This calling seems to permeate every aspect of their being and compels them to seek for the meaning and truth of their earthly experience. Around these children there is an uneasiness and an uncertainty as to what the next step in their personal development and in their life's direction should be.

Rest assured, however, for there is a purpose. There is a Divine intent in the calling which you sense and from which you have acted. Within this wave of change there is a higher purpose. Allow this truth to help you to see more clearly. Let the understanding of this dispel your fears. Allow your compassion to dispel your seeming lack of sympathy for others and allow your growing reliance on your connectedness with the Divine to help loosen the tethers that bind you to the things of the earth.

For the truth will indeed set you free.

All may minister in this time, but to do so, all must strive to prepare the way - first in themselves and then in others - to be channels of forces that will save, regenerate, and sustain the earth in relationship to the Creator or the First Cause.

And how will this way be prepared in you? What must you eliminate? What must you obliterate?

The things of the darkness that lie within you. Hatred. Anger. Passion. Pride. Selfishness. All the things of the earth that so often impregnate the sons of the earth and hinder them from becoming sons of the Most High.

This is the time that has been heralded by the prophets, seers, and sages of all ages. It is a time of transition. It is a time of testing. It is a time of choosing in whom and in what you will place your faith?

And in this time, there are many of these children who have already chosen.

They have heard the golden sceptre ring within their hearts and minds. They have prepared the way in themselves to hear the call and have responded. They are ready to take on the task, to run the race, and to endure until the end.

These children who are bonded in a love of the truth and a love of the earth, have come to aid in this time of transition. They have come to allow love, peace, and the Divine laws to manifest through them and into the earth. They have come to help find a way for others to ride this wave of transition to the shores of a heavenly home upon the earth. They have come to experience peace and love and then to turn and extend their hands to those who continue to battle with the storm-tossed seas.

It is these children who seek the light who have a covenant with the earth and the Divine. It is these who have come for a purpose, a mission, which resides in their hearts and minds and souls.

They come with these desires: To hear their Father's voice; to align themselves with Will Divine; to help their brother and sister souls wend their way into closer relationship with the First Cause.

And it is to these children of the light that we CALL.

## 1.2 EARTH AS A BATTLEGROUND

The earth, in this time of transition, is a battleground. This is the Final Crusade where the division and the duality between the forces of light and the forces of darkness are being drawn apart. From the blending of the light of truth and the darkness of dismay, there is a separation, a clarification, a distillation so that man can move from a state of ignorance to recognition of the interplay of these two forces in his life.

Man may then clearly choose which force he will serve.

The plight that has plagued man's evolution into the mind of his Maker has been forgetfulness. Man has forgotten that he possesses a soul and that it resides with him and within him.

For the past 130 years, or since the Industrial Age, man has revered the works of man in preference and in deference to the works of the Divine. He has placed his faith in science and technology, in a type of humanism, and in the institutions that he himself has created.

These beliefs have trapped and imprisoned man in earthly consciousness. His thinking has become grounded. His being is permeated with a sense of the mundane, acceptance of mediocrity, and a feeling of hopelessness.

He is caught in grief, anger, resentment, and a deepening sorrow about what he sees. There is within him a negative fatalism, cynicism, and an all-prevailing sense of loss and helplessness in the movement of earthly events through his life.

As a result, man has negated his own imagination and his own ability to reach heavenward and partake of the light of the Divine. For love is healing and love is truth and mankind, by his own personal choices, has begun to extinguish this Divine light within the earth.

Man possesses the ability to be a co-creator with the Divine, but so often has chosen to pursue only his own limited understanding. This limited thinking has led to the pollution of his own heart, mind, and body and through association, those of his earthly brothers and sisters.

And as he has done it to himself, so is he polluting the soils, the waters, and the airs of mother earth.

Man is comprised of body, mind, and soul forces that are in intimate relationship with one another. No one of these can be affected without affecting the others in kind.

This earthly pollution has affected the body or the physical expression of man. The supply of foods, waters, and airs in and around the earth, are all contaminated with excesses of carbon. As man ingests these pollutants, his body is toxified and his natural ability to detoxify or eliminate these carbons is experiencing strain and difficulty.

The physical imbalance in the body of man is resulting in increased incidence of cancer and heart disease. The imbalance in the fluids of man is resulting in increased incidence of diabetes, kidney disease, and liver dysfunctions. His body has become weakened and lies open to a myriad of other illnesses and diseases, both named and, as yet, unnamed.

The impact of these pollutants on the physical body of man has a corresponding impact on his mind and his emotions.

He will have an inability to think, focus, or concentrate clearly or with duration. His ability to reason will be greatly impaired. His desire or wish to dedicate effort to finding the truth will be diminished.

The impact of these pollutants on his emotional body will not allow him to clearly feel or sense his relationship with self or with those others who will aid him in awakening to his soul's purpose. Relationships that should never have been formed, will be formed in his emotional ignorance. Relationships in which the learning is completed, will be clung to whether they be of an intimate or vocational nature. Relationships which should be formed for a greater learning or purpose, will pass by him, unrecognized and unseen.

This has resulted in a tearing or a breaking down of the very fabric of society. The nuclear family will be broken in a variety of ways. Communities will be fragmented, fractured, and confused and will be rendered mentally, emotionally, or physically bankrupt. Look at the plight of New York, London, Moscow, and Bejiing. All of these are experiencing dissolution on one or more of these levels.

This breakdown of the community is causing a breakdown and attempted reformation of political structures. It is ocurring from the villages and towns even unto the nations. In Eastern Europe, Russia, China, Africa, and in India. All over the face of the earth there is a cracking and a fracturing of these man-made structures.

The pollution of thought and belief is moving into all areas of earthly endeavor.

Governments are unable to devise solutions that are in balance and in harmony with this wave of transition.

They cling, almost helplessly, to the status-quo and act out of alignment with their thoughts and beliefs.

The destabilization of governmental thought is, in turn, reflected in the realms of world finance and economics. The dominance of a type of humanism is excluding the active participation of the Divine. Currencies and their institutions will be dissolved, re-established, and then dissolved again.

All aspects of the globe will be profoundly impacted. And the Institutions of man will be shaken to their very foundations.

Scattered amongst these institutions, there are those who see this battle, this Final Crusade, as an opportunity for meaningful change. There are those who, embodying the seeds of truth, simply know that in order to save themselves, their community, and this planet called earth, there must be change.

Around these awakened ones is a sense of urgency and a sense of purpose. They have been placed in all walks of earthly life and in all manner of earthly structures. They are the teachers, the healers, the leaders, the ministers, and the workers who simply know that if mankind's motivation is not altered, that if mankind's thinking is not changed, that if man's thoughts and actions are not aligned with Divine intent...then the path that mankind walks is the path to death and darkness.

These are the ones known as the children who seek the light and they are being called into service for this, the Final Crusade.

## 1.3 THE VIEW FROM THE HEAVENS

The etheric plane is that dimension of consciousness wherein reside beings of light, the messengers of God, and the angels of the First Cause. This is the place to which all holy men and women aspire and the place from which all prophets and teachers of the truth obtain their nurturance.

Through this heavenly realm, and at the desire of the First Cause, the earth was formed as an experimental and an experiential planet of love. It was a place to which beings from other dimensions and other states of knowing could descend and assume the garments of materiality and experience the challenges afforded to them by the flesh.

Few planets exist in the universes on which awareness is so confining and so limiting and so ponderous.

In the beginning, in the higher realms, the earth was known as the pearl within the oyster of God's hand. The light from this pearl beckoned to those beings in higher dimensions to come and partake of the challenges offered by this three-dimensional expression.

The heavenly experiment involved the giving of choice to mankind as to whether he would move and evolve into limited earthly understanding or to move - with his physical vehicle - into greater harmony and understanding and relationship with his image of God.

From the heavens, the earth emitted a heavenly golden-silver light and a green ring illuminated and girdled the globe.

Now the pollution of man's fleshly beliefs has limited the emergence of the earthly light into the heavenly spheres. Man's consciousness has encircled the earth with a sickly grayness resulting from his sense of loss, grief, and bitterness towards others. In this way mankind and the earth are severing their connectedness with the Divine.

Many are being called by those in the etheric realms from all different and varied dimensions to aid in this time of transition.

**The Calling of the Children of Light, then, is not only a call to those of and in the earth, but is a CALLING in the heavens as well.**

When viewed from the etheric, the face of the earth is riddled with varying concentrations of darkness, a darkness caused by mankind's dismay, feelings of isolation, and a sense of disconnectedness from the Divine. The very soul of mankind is almost paralyzed by the barriers man himself has created, and so those in the etheric stand and watch.

**When we in the etheric look upon the earthly-framework, we can see pinpoints of great darkness.**

**Mexico City is tremendously dark.**

**Japan is beginning to move into the darkness of its own making. Technology has hardened the hearts of man within that island-continent, and will cause a rippling and a movement of energy around the island which will not disappear until the island-continent itself disappears.**

**In viewing Europe, the experiments with atomic and sub-atomic particles that are directed to the creation of a new form of energy from energy itself, has caused a darkness. Their scientific curiousity has precluded**

divinity, and therein is the darkness within Europe. There is great concern for Paris, the lower part of England, the northern and western fringes of France, and the greater part of Germany.

New York and Los Angeles have elements of tremendous darkness within them. There is a seediness, a sense of true loss, and total confusion and chaos. Even though there are lights within those areas that shine out in an attempt to aid and lighten and give a sense of purpose, there is great confusion. This chaotic sense of loss is causing a type of blackness in those areas.

The areas of Taiwan, Hong Kong, Southern China, Vietnam, Thailand, and Cambodia are suffering. The fringes of these areas (along the waters) are blackened with a sense of loss.

There is concern for different parts of India. The area of greatest concern is in the heart or the very core of India. Although higher topographically, this area is experiencing a type of heart-throb that is causing a breaking within and below the earth. It is like a caving in that is occurring there.

This place that has been the height of spiritual knowledge in the earth, the library of the earth from the earliest times, is beginning - because of it's lack of growing awareness and it's lack of desire to reach beyond the stars and into the mind of God - to experience a sense of depression and it is affecting the very heart of India.

In Africa, there is such confusion and dismay and decay, that - for those who reside there - at the best they will experience great demoralization.

Russia and its fellow states are finding disaster within. Continual breaking of that unit will force dissolutions, reformations, and dissolutions again.

*Oracles of Light ,November 1991*

Man's attempts to find a solution to his mental and physical pollution are failing. Oftentimes, the light that needs to enter the earth from the heavens and the light that needs to be emitted cannot find it's way through the barriers of belief. The result is that even the animals and vegetation are being impacted and are dying. All appears to be in a state of decay and confusion.

But those in the etheric realms are present, not just to observe this earthly drama as it unfolds, but to give aid and to give love in ways that are tangible.

When those in the etheric see a need, sense a desperation, a situation of unhealthiness, a situation of dismay, they send their light and their love, the energy that they carry within their own spirits, to those who are in need.

Even now, great shafts of light are being sent into and through the cracks in this mental and physical cloudiness in an attempt to lift and enlighten man's polluted thinking. They guide and listen to the hearts of men. They constantly strive to communicate with souls that are caught in this physical web and the maze of confused human thinking.

The opportunity for mankind and the children of the light at this time is that any assistance that can be given to those individuals - at whatever level of learning or understanding they may find themselves - will be given.

**IF ONE BUT CALLS...IF ONE SIMPLY ASKS...THERE WILL BE AN ANSWER.**

There will be confirmation and validation given to each who asks. There will be illumination given to those who question, for those who look for the light and the experience of God in the earth.

This is the GIFT and this is the PROMISE in this TIME.

# 1.4    THE SHIFT IN PLANETARY CONSCIOUSNESS

The SHIFT in planetary consciousness is the movement of the consciousness of mankind from the third to the fourth dimension. There will be a tremendous change from the limitations of three-dimensional awareness to the expansive freedom of the realms of thoughts and ideas. It is an evolutionary step in man's earthly nature and will bring with it a closer relationship for him and his planet to the Divine.

There is a tremendous concentration of light and energy pouring into the earth from the heavens. The light and the love is in response to the etherics' desire to aid those in the earthly framework and to give only light and to give only love.

At the same time, the energy of man and his learning is being confined to the earth by his self-created, barrier-like beliefs. In a sense, the energy he generates is being held and reflected back upon himself.

As a consequence of these two forces, the spirit of truth and the spirit of darkness, the efforts of the heavens and the efforts of mankind, the earth is becoming an inflamed crucible of emotional and spiritual experience. The purpose of these events is to aid in purging the weight of corruption and disharmony from the very soul of mankind.

This time of transition will be a time of extremes wherein time itself will be quickened and compressed. Emotions will be heightened and the earth, and those who inhabit her surface, will begin to SPIN ever faster in an effort to throw off the weight of their physical and mental pollution.

For the children of the light, each will experience the quickening that results from this spin in different ways. Their beliefs will be rapidly re-examined, formulated, discarded, and reformulated. Their relationships will be severed, redefined, and rejoined in different and unique ways. Their vocations will be questioned and they will begin to move in different directions. They will begin to express different talents, abilities, and gifts that may have lain dormant within them.

They will be exposed fully to all that is negative and desultory, both within and outside of themselves, and they will be fully exposed to the light of truth and the love of the Divine so that each may CHOOSE.

Many souls now in earthly expression will also choose the darkness. These souls would have been so negated in their thinking that they would have forgotten how to even so much as look for the love of the Divine or search for their God. It is these souls who will be taken by famine, pestilence, and disease. It is these souls who will be limited by their own beliefs and doubts and fears. It is these souls who will cling desperately to what they had known, to the institutions that they had worshipped, and will perish in this time of transition even as the many, self-centered creations of man shall perish.

Know, however, that those who reach for Him will touch Him. Those who search for Him will find Him. This is the promise and the fulfillment of His covenant in this time.

For millennia, the spirit of truth has called to the hearts and minds of men. But in this time, the intensity and the frequency of this calling has dramatically increased.

Since August of 1987, when the heavens and the prophecies of man were in harmony and convergence, the call to love and light has been directed from the heavens onto the earth. In August of 1989, there was a second and more profound calling or shift in planetary consciousness that stimulated the alignment of many earthly souls. In August of 1991 there was a third.

Every two years, then, there were shifts or "bumps" in consciousness which had, and are having, a profound impact on the earthly-framework. These "bumps" are effecting and affecting man's concentration and learning and are providing an ability for a tremendous amount of information to flow to him. Great opportunities for rapid growth are being given to many for each year in these two year cycles are equivalent to 10 years of previous earthly existence (as time was in 1960).

The consequence of these cycles of change is a tremendous stress, through the resulting actions and reactions, on the very framework of the earth.

From August of 1991 to August of 1992, there will be a relative calming of the rate of change. This is to allow some stabilization to take place in the lives of men from all they have endured up until this time.

Then, in August of 1992, there will be yet another shift in consciousness and each year beyond this time will be likened to 20 years of previous earthly existence. A sign or omen of these times will be a profound change in earth's climate that will be followed by tremendous winds.

It will be a time of great turmoil and tribulation for mankind, and - because of the awakened consciousness of many of the children of the light and the desire by the Divine that no soul should be lost - this time of testing will be shortened for all.

In these ensuing years, all that you have placed between you and your image of God will be removed. All that you have held sacred and dear will be questioned. All that you felt yourself to be, you will no longer be. All this will occur so that your true nature as His children will be given the opportunity to manifest.

## 1.5 CREATION and EVOLUTION

In the beginning, there was the darkness that knew itself to be itself and, contained within this darkness, there was an awareness of its ability to give illumination unto itself.

Within that darkness that thought, and hummed, and was aware of itself, there existed the Great Mind and the understanding of illumination, the understanding of enlightenment, the understanding of the power of love and the force that was contained within it.

In that understanding of illumination there was contained an inner and eternal light. The light always was and always existed within the depths of the darkness.

As this light, this motion, this electricity, this illumination took form, it found that there was an ability to move out from it's own centeredness and to begin to expand.

God desired to share the movement and expansion of His light. He desired to allow others, who would be as His companions, to sing in His song of creation, so that He made souls in his own image to help and to participate in the unfolding of the universes and to aid in His desire to transform the darkness into light.

And these souls were as a separate, co-creative vibration, and yet one with the greater light of the Divine.

The darkness would experience a sense of newness from the light as it expanded into itself. The light moved to the furthest reaches of the darkness to illuminate it, to bond with it, to align with that all-knowing awareness that was present in the darkness.

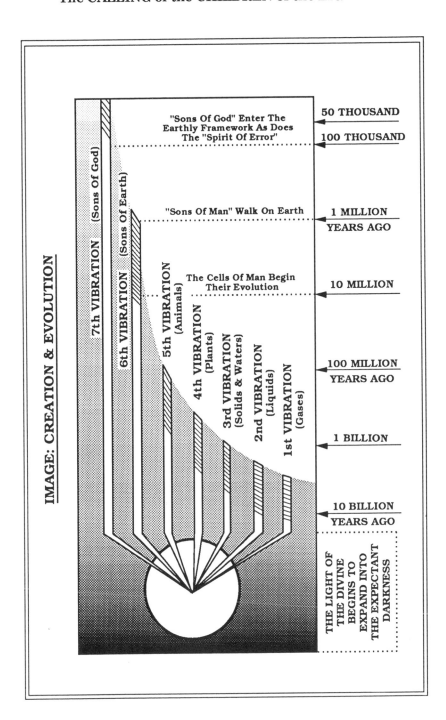

IMAGE: CREATION & EVOLUTION

7th VIBRATION   (Sons Of God)

6th VIBRATION   (Sons Of Earth)

5th VIBRATION (Animals)

4th VIBRATION (Plants)

3rd VIBRATION (Solids & Waters)

2nd VIBRATION (Liquids)

1st VIBRATION (Gases)

"Sons Of God" Enter The Earthly Framework As Does The "Spirit Of Error"

"Sons Of Man" Walk On Earth

The Cells Of Man Begin Their Evolution

50 THOUSAND

100 THOUSAND

1 MILLION YEARS AGO

10 MILLION

100 MILLION YEARS AGO

1 BILLION

10 BILLION YEARS AGO

THE LIGHT OF THE DIVINE BEGINS TO EXPAND INTO THE EXPECTANT DARKNESS

And as this light moved from its own centeredness, it moved in soft and gentle waves. It moved in vibrations of energy and consciousness. The light carried within itself illumination, power, and the ability for co-creation. It carried with it the ability to move into the darkness, to move it aside and to ingest it within itself so that the darkness could become light.

So that Great Mind - the Mighty of all Mighties - allowed that flow, that vibration from its own centeredness and the very core of it's own awareness, to move and to express itself in a different way.

From this great power there is a movement of rays - for vibration, energy, and light will often move in rays. And these rays are likened to the mighty arms of God that reach out and move in the awareness that the darkness will be consumed by the light, but that there is an ability for the darkness and the light to co-exist.

As these rays of light from its own centeredness moved into all the corners and all the awareness of that which simply was the expectant darkness, there was an understanding that the differences in vibration would create a new application of the ability for co-creation.

Within these two initial vibrations, there arose the ability for the light to blend with the darkness and to form gaseous matter. That which was to occur, did occur in this way.

The great hands of God took the light and the darkness and blended them together, and warmed them, and this gaseous matter became the planets, the moons, and the stars. And these became places where the different occurrences and experiences of God could manifest in a new way.

And this was the beginning, in this universe, of the movement of the rays of God.

The earth was formed in this way. Then another vibration moved and gave the earth its atmosphere. Then still another vibration moved and gave an opportunity for the waters to exist. Then there was a sense of plant life, and a third vibration moved to accommodate this desire which is the co-creative nature of God Himself.

Then there was the fish, the fowl, and the animal life as these vibrations moved onto the earth. And contained within it all, was an energized spark of Divine awareness. One cell divided into two and so on such that the pattern of animal evolution began. The vibration itself created its own awareness and its own state of consciousness from all its different kinds of vibrations.

Herein lies the key to understanding. The tree and the human are both in the consciousness of the one great mind. But these two exist at different vibrational understandings of that consciousness. Both have the ability to be aware, but each formulates their understanding of their relationship to the Creator in a different way due to their consciousness and their state of being.

The earth, as it had moved in evolution from gas, liquid, solid, plant, and animal life, was now ready for the introduction of mankind.

About ten million years ago, this sixth and wondrous ray of God continued its movement into the earth with yet another vibration, one that was more complex, more energized, that allowed itself to exert a different kind of awareness on the earth.

And this sixth vibration formed the cells that would mold themselves into human form. Thus, mankind did not evolve from animals, but was a separate creation.

Man and woman were created and would become known as the sons and daughters of the earth or the sons of man. The sons of God in consciousness, but made from the soil and the waters and the elements of the earth.

They were to walk in grace upon the earth while being fashioned from it. This Divine experiment was to determine if the consciousness of the earth could join with that which was worthy of governing that consciousness, namely, the consciousness of the Divine.

The result of this experiment was a sense of dispassionate awareness. The sons of man became so unaware of their spiritual intent and of their link with God, that there needed to be a quickening of their consciousness and assistance given by the Great Mind, the Great Love, and the power of all the universes.

And then a different kind of vibration was injected into the earth and it is this vibration that needs to be clarified.

## THE ENTRANCE OF THE
## CHILDREN OF THE LIGHT

The mighty rays move out from the center in co-creative spirit and in awe. With each particular ray, and within each soul that exists within that ray as a spark or speck of light, there is a power of innate and infinite ability to know all things and be one with the mind of God.

Each soul-speck has the ability to understand Divine intent and to act as an instrument of Divine intent.

When that soul-speck is in existence in the etheric realm, and especially when it has not experienced any other dimensional awareness (such as three-dimensional earthly existence), there is a very clear consciousness that everything moves in love. Everything is expressed in joy.

Light is simply the vehicle. Energy is the motion. Frequency is a part of that energized motion and so there is a wonder and a state of rapture in the spirit.

If you examine that soul-speck it can rightly be called spirit in the etheric. It can also be called a light being. This is especially true of those souls who never incarnated into other dimensions and remained within that initial state of spiritual awareness. They can be called, and should be equated, with a light being or angel.

The seventh vibration and the spirit within that same moved further and further into a different awareness of consciousness. Closer and closer this light approached the earthly framework.

When the awareness arose that the sons of earth were experiencing difficulty (and understand that the sons of earth possess the spark of the Creator within them, but there was a different vibration and they had forgotten their connection with the Almighty), there arose an understanding by the Great Mind that further assistance must be given unto the earth.

And thus, the seventh ray, this seventh vibration would become known as the children of the light. These children understood that love and light and healing was to be given to the earthly planet for it was beginning to forget its link with the Divine in a number of different ways.

This spirit moved towards the earth and incarnated from the very earliest times to aid and to be of service to those who were as the sons of earth.

About 75,000 to 100,000 years ago, during the rise of the Lemurian civilization on the earth, there occurred two falls in the awareness and experience of the sons of God.

One was as a fall from grace in the heavens and one was as a fall from knowledge and understanding as the children of the light strove to help their brother and sister souls in the earth.

## THE FALL OF THE SONS OF GOD IN THE HEAVENS

As the Divine rays began to expand, soul-specks manifested. Some soul-specks chose to illuminate the darkness. Others chose to directly experience and to aid in the unfolding and evolution of the various universes while still others desired to remain within the Divine vibrational awareness.

Those soul-specks who chose to remain and constantly behold the face and hear the voice of the First Cause are called light beings, spirit beings, or angels.

The angelic realms are those that exist closest to the Divine. Those who inhabit these realms are known, in man's understanding, as Archangels.

The Archangels have the ability to be the *messengers* or voice of the Divine. They are as *heralds* that move with ease through all the dimensions, delivering Divine messages with harmony and consistency between all the universes and all the realms of manifested and unmanifested creation. They are as *observers* of the Divine plan of evolution and act as intermediaries, intercessors, and spokesman of and to the Divine for the various universes and dimensions with which they have been entrusted. They are as *stewards*, embodying and ensuring that the Divine laws of the universes are maintained. And they carry within them the co-creative power, wisdom, and the knowledge of the knowledge that resides in - and forms the very core of - the Divine.

And one such Archangel was, and is still known, as Lucifer.

Lucifer was a beloved companion of the Divine. He carried out his heavenly duties with love and grace, so much so, that he became more than a messenger, servant, or steward of the Divine, but became a true friend and one with the Divine focus.

And his beauty and nobility exceeded all those who had inhabited the angelic realms.

As the Divine plan patiently unfolded, Lucifer began to grow in belief that the light and the power within him was his own. He began to grow to love himself and his achievements just slightly more than he loved the Divine. He began to grow in a desire to control, manipulate, and influence the purposes, thoughts, and patterns of other souls. And he wanted his messages to be carried to the farthest reaches of the universe in preference and deference to the messages from the Divine.

Then finally, Lucifer came to desire to no longer be a servant of the Living God, but a god and a law unto himself.

It was self-interest in opposition to Divine-interest. It was selfishness as opposed to selflessness. It was self-aggrandizement as opposed to honoring and glorifying the Divine. And it was power that had been misdirected, misused, and had gone astray.

From the beginning, each soul-speck was given the ability to choose how it would co-creatively mold and fashion the light of the Divine. In the heavens, this choice is made with full knowledge and understanding of the soul's relationship to the Divine, whereas for earth-bound souls, it is often exercised in ignorance, limitation, and a sense of separation.

Lucifer had *knowingly chosen* to oppose Divine-intent in preference to his own, self-centered intent and, in so doing, gave birth to the spirit of rebellion.

God became aware of this emerging disharmony within His song of creation and called Lucifer to Him and asked of Lucifer why he had manifested this spirit of dischord?

Lucifer replied that he only desired to become more god-like. 'Was this not what the Creator desired for all souls? Should we not all be striving to become better co-creative instruments?', he had argued. 'Do I not need to experiment and excercise my ability to choose how your Divine light can and should be manifested?'

As with all His children, God saw the true intent and purposes in Lucifer's heart, but never-the-less, allowed Lucifer's choice of opposing the Divine plan to manifest in certain regions of creation.

All those in the heavens were warned of the difficulties that they could encounter in returning to alignment with the Divine if they were to follow Lucifer's ways. Then, once apprised of the dangers and the pitfalls, all were given a choice whether to be in opposition to or in harmony with the Divine plan.

God had decreed, in permitting and allowing the manifestation of Lucifer's spirit of rebellion, that only certain specific universes and dimensions were to be as Satan's playground. To ensure that there would be compliance with this Divine commandment, God set in opposition to Lucifer that one known as the Archangel Michael to monitor and to maintain His error-limiting law.

Then Lucifer descended, calling to him all those soul-specks that had chosen to align themselves with his intent, into the lower vibrational states of awareness.

In this way, the sons of God fell from the grace and light of the Divine and Lucifer became the prince of darkness, the lord of the underworld, or the Satan for certain universes that existed in three-dimensional awareness.

## THE HOLY BATTLE IN THE HEAVENS

Now Lucifer - being of angelic nature, retained the ability to move through and travel between all of the dimensions and universes, but was restricted by Divine edict to influencing and spreading his message of rebellion to only the lower dimensions. But his desire to spread his message in preference to the Divine began to grow and he formulated a plan to move his awareness towards the forbidden, higher dimensions.

Michael became aware of Lucifer's intent and met his awareness in that place known as the fifth dimension. There followed a tremendous battle, the effects of which reverberated throughout all of creation.

The sons of the earth saw this battle in the skies as varied colored lights, movements of the stars, and brilliant explosions that filled them with terror, wonder, and concern. And the memory of this battle is indelibly ingrained in mankind's collective unconscious.

The forces of light that were with Michael prevailed against the forces of darkness and eliminated Lucifer's influence from the fifth dimension.

For know that Michael is the Lord of the Way and ever stands as the guardian and protector of all those on the earth who experience the change that accompanies the seeking of the light of the Divine. The Way is through the Christ Consciousness or the mind of the Divine. But the Lord and the Law of the Way is that one known as Michael.

The remnant of this heavenly battle between the spirit of rebellion and the spirit of truth was the destruction of the fifth planet in every system and in every universe that was given under the influence of Lucifer.

Thus, it came to pass that the spirit of error and the spirit of truth would co-exist with one another on the earthly-framework. Both, in their essence, are of the Divine and therefore one with that same, but each is of a differing intent.

## THE FALL OF THE SONS OF GOD IN THE EARTH

The Divine had forseen the possible descent into the earthly-framework of those souls who had chosen the darkness and the retarding impact they would have on the evolution of mankind's consciousness. He was aware that a positive influence was needed, not only to awaken man's forgetfulness of the Divine, but to balance the forces of darkness that would seek to maintain man's state of ignorance.

Thus, in the Lemurian experience nearly 100,000 years ago, the sons of God or the children of the light would descend, commune, guide, and experience manifestation with the sons of the earth.

As time passed, a few of these children moved into the rocks, and vegetation, and experienced the sons and daughters of men.

In this intermixing there was a great confusion, aided and encouraged by the presence of the spirit of error, and what resulted were aberrations and abominations on the earth. There was the blending of the human form with the minerals, soils, and animals such that there were giants, dwarfs, and humans with mixtures of horns, hooves, feathers, and tails.

And this was the FALL from knowledge and understanding of the sons of God in the earth as they strove to aid those others to remember their Divine heritage.

The great confusion resulting from the blending of the sons of God with the daughters of men caused God even greater concern. For now He had lost -in this blending - a vibration that was beloved and possessed of a co-creative intent that could aid in moving the darkness into a state of light.

Upon the instruction of the Divine, a tremendous mass of the children of the light began to move and explore in and around the earth. These were as guides or spiritually aware beings who simply observed the development of the earth for millennia.

After some time, when all was in readiness, many children incarnated and were caught by the mundane issues. Even upon their release from incarnation, they would still carry the understanding of the confusion that they experienced on the earth.

The children then withdrew for a time and formulated an understanding that another approach was needed to heal, transform, and move the unconscious state on the earth into a more conscious state of awareness of the Divine.

## THE FINAL JOURNEY

About 25,000 years ago, near the final ending of Lemuria and the beginning of the rise of Atlantis, these souls who were the children of the light, entered into the earthly-framework with a singular purpose of helping to awaken the light of the Divine within man.

Each soul that entered the earth, split itself into two aspects; creative and receptive, yin and yang, male and female, to more closely approximate and align with the sons and daughters of men.

These twin souls, as they would become known, took the flame of their one soul and placed it into the light of two, consciously aware beings as they incarnated on the earth.

And one such soul that broke from within itself, became Amilius and Lilith in the land known as Atlantis. It became Adam and Eve in the garden known as Eden. And it became Jesus and Mary in the holy land known as Palestine.

## 1.6 THE CHILDREN OF ALL AGES

These two paths and forces known as the sons of God and the sons of rebellion, the children of the light and the sons and daughters of darkness, danced throughout the recent history of man's sojourn on the earth. One force striving to aid and one force striving to impede the Divine evolutionary plan.

The dance, in its essence, was the descent or involution of the light, love, and truth of the Divine into man's conscious awareness and the ascent or evolution of man's earthly nature into a clearer understanding of his relationship with the First Cause.

For know that the light of truth and love has always been the same - for God is the same, yesterday, today, and tomorrow - but what has changed throughout history is man's understanding and application of this one truth.

Man, in reflecting on his tenure upon the earth, has continually sought to understand the meaning of the events of his earthly existence in the context of space and time. What man often seems to forget is that time is simply an idea and a means through which the earthly drama of his soul may be enacted and remembered.

In the heavenly realms there is no time. From the Divine perspective, what is important is not the sequence of earthly events nor speculation as to their cause, but whether the lessons needed by the soul were learned.

Many ancient civilizations understood that the rhythm, position, and movements of the bodies that comprise the universe and the movement of man's awareness were related in some fashion. They understood that there was a correspondence between the seasons, migrations, and processions of the earthly, lunar, planetary, solar, and star cycles and the situations, circumstances, and opportunities mankind faced in his earthly sojourns.

For it is truth that all are indeed one. As it is above...so is it reflected below. As it is without...so can it be seen and found to be within.

Each individual's thoughts, feelings, and actions impact the very spirit or soul of mankind. And in turn, the collective thoughts, feelings, and actions of the soul of mankind impacts the individual.

Life is a continuum and no event or individual can be viewed correctly in isolation. Just as each event that an individual experiences is built upon the choices he has made in the past, each cycle of learning in which mankind may find himself has resulted from the collective choices made by the soul of mankind in the past.

Thus, for one to grasp the fuller meaning of the present age or cycle of man, one must seek to know and understand that which came before it.

### THE AGES AND THE CYCLES OF MAN

Prior to the final destruction of Atlantis around 12,500 years ago, an age of man was comprised of about 25,000 years. For half the age the soul of mankind would descend into closer relationship with his earthly nature and for the other half of the age, man would ascend into closer relationship and manifestation of his Divine nature.

Within each 12,500 year period, there were four cycles of learning that characterized man's state of awareness.

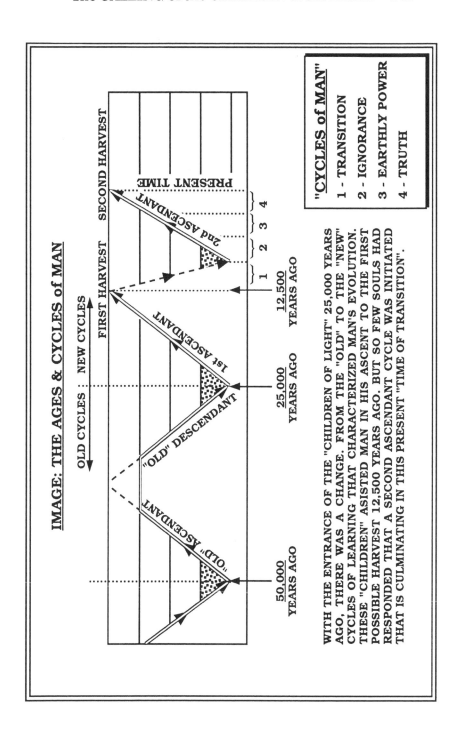

## IMAGE: THE AGES & CYCLES of MAN

WITH THE ENTRANCE OF THE "CHILDREN OF LIGHT" 25,000 YEARS AGO, THERE WAS A CHANGE. FROM THE "OLD" TO THE "NEW" CYCLES OF LEARNING THAT CHARACTERIZED MAN'S EVOLUTION. THESE "CHILDREN" ASISTED MAN IN HIS ASCENT TO THE FIRST POSSIBLE HARVEST 12,500 YEARS AGO. BUT SO FEW SOULS HAD RESPONDED THAT A SECOND ASCENDANT CYCLE WAS INITIATED THAT IS CULMINATING IN THIS PRESENT "TIME OF TRANSITION".

The first was the cycle of materiality or ignorance. The second was the cycle of growing earthly power and awareness. The third was the cycle of mental development that carried with it a sense of inner and outer exploration. And the fourth was the age of growing awareness of scientific and spiritual truth.

The children of the light physically entered the earthly-framework about 25,000 years ago when the soul of mankind was in a cycle of ignorance and materiality. They walked, shared, and experienced the ascendant cycle from earthly power, to mind, to science and spirituality.

And it was this last cycle of growing awareness of truth in science and spirituality that most closely approximates the cycle which man is re-experiencing today.

As in this time, the call resounded in the heavens and the earth to gather those who sought the light. As in this time, the etheric realms began the spin to quicken and to aid in the cleansing of the planetary consciousness. As in this time, the forces of light and darkness were divided for what was believed to be the Final Crusade. As in this time, there was the potential for planetary destruction through the misuse of the powers and laws of nature.

But so few souls responded to the calling, that it was decided in the heavens to provide another opportunity for the sons of God and the sons of the earth to extricate themselves from mundane forgetfulness and awaken to their Divine heritage.

So mankind experienced a change in the gradual descent and ascent that had characterized the cycles of learning up to that point in time and the soul of mankind descended into the depths of ignorance to ascend and climb and prepare yet again for the opportunity to evolve from third to fourth dimensional awareness.

## THE FINAL ASCENT OF THE SOUL OF MANKIND

The battle that led to the destruction of Atlantis was the battle between spirituality and science. It was a conflict between the knowledge of the personal power of the Divine that resides within the very core of man and the power and energy that can be viewed to exist outside of man.

The desire in the heavens was to blend and merge these two awarenesses, to move man upwards towards the next step in his evolution, and to harvest all those souls who had awakened to their relationship with the Divine.

What occurred, however, was the use of scientific knowledge and power for self-interest by those in positions of authority with the consequence of overwhelming chaos, confusion, and destruction of all that was.

And all those in the heavens wept at the loss of this opportunity for the soul of mankind.

The final destruction was followed by a cycle of transition where many strove to preserve the knowledge of Atlantis. This desire for preservation was overshadowed by a growing descent into darkness and dismay. This cycle of ignorance was followed by a growing sense of earthly stability, power, and creativity and, over the past 3000 years or so, mankind has witnessed the re-emergence of the seeking of truth through science and spirituality.

The *"Cycle of Transition"* (10,600 to 7500 BC) was a period of preservation and growing pre-occupation with physical survival.

Those of the Atlantean awareness who had forseen the possibility of the cataclysm, made efforts to preserve the spiritual and scientific knowledge in various regions of the earth.

The Atlanteans had established colonies from the northern fringes of what is now Europe to the southern ends of the Americas, and many identical bodies of information were transported to what was believed to be safe harbours in those colonies in the hope that a few would survive into this present time.

The colony to which many Atlanteans fled was in Egypt in the place known in this day as Gizeh. There, the children of the light constructed a "symbol" which would serve to call the peoples throughout this ascendant age into remembrance of how the Divine could manifest in the earth. That "symbol" is the Great Pyramid of Gizeh and, in and around and within the structures built there with Atlantean knowledge, there can be found one of the bodies of information that awaits the proper time for discovery and revelation.

As time passed, the efforts of preservation gave way to a profound sense of the loss of what had and could have been and the social structures slowly gave way to decay.

The majority of the peoples who had survived the shifting of the poles of the earth, the sinking and rising of lands, and the massive movements and changing courses of the waters, strove to preserve themselves by adopting a nomadic awareness and they moved in accordance with the migrations of earth, water, seasons, and the beasts of the earth.

Thus, much that had been Atlantean in thought and manifestation was swallowed by the movements of the

## IMAGE: THE GREAT PYRAMID

GOD

SPIRITUAL

(PURPOSE)

Fire

TRUTH   MENTAL   (THOUGHT)   Air   "IAM"   Water   (DESIRE)   EMOTIONAL   LOVE

Earth

(GOALS)

PHYSICAL

LAW

THE PYRAMID WAS BUILT AS A CALL TO REMEMBRANCE OF ALL
THE EARTH-BOUND SOULS IN THIS FINAL ASCENDANT CYCLE OF
MAN. WHEN UNFOLDED, MAN'S FOURFOLD NATURE AS HE
EXPRESSED IN THE EARTH IS RELATED TO THE DIVINE. FOR
GOD IS LOVE, TRUTH, AND LAW.

earth, washed away by the waters, or blown by the winds of change from the recollections of man in this cycle of transition.

The *"Cycle of Ignorance"* (7500 to 4400 BC) was a time of growing inner and outer darkness. The past was gradually forgotten and the veil of forgetfulness grew heavier and served to contract man's conscious awareness.

The nomadic movements of the peoples continued in response to the continuing instability of the earthly framework. The ability to communicate with all the races through a common language - as in the Atlantean time - was severed with the growing isolation and formation of local dialects.

In this cycle, there was a lack of prophetic leaders, sages, or visionaries. The duality that strove to become oneness in the final days of Atlantis, degenerated into the worship of many gods and mankind's Divine awareness was burdened with ritualism, superstition, and animal and human sacrifice.

And mankind's awareness drew ever closer to the earth upon which he dwelt.

The *"Cycle of Earthly Power"* (4400 to 1250 BC) was a period of emerging stability, creativity, and reinterpretation of man's relationship to the universe.

The earth had become more stable and predictable in terms of the seasons, the movement of the soils, and the position of the waters. Although the majority of mankind continued to follow nomadic ways, there arose pockets of those who desired familiarity and stability and, in a sense, anchored themselves to the earth by establishing communities.

As the framework of these communities solidified, more time was devoted to thought and the creative expression of those thoughts. There arose artists and artisans, sculptors and builders, painters and those who fashioned pottery.

And to protect and defend what man had wrought and built, the art of warriorship re-emerged into man's conscious awareness.

The isolation and separation that had characterized the cycle of darkness, gave way in this time to a sense of exploration. Attempts were made to discover and rediscover what lay beyond the perimeters of the existing communities by land and by sea.

In the heart of India, where resides the library of the earth, efforts were made to collect, transcribe, and reinterpret the knowledge and truths from the ancient civilizations of Lemuria and Atlantis. History, philosophy, and the exploration of the truth that could be found within, emerged again into man's awareness.

The final cycle in the ascent of man is the *"Cycle of Truth"* (1250 BC to the present).

In this cycle of learning, man gained the ability to deal with abstract ideas and concepts. There arose a growing sense that life, in its essence, was good and that there was a hope that it would continue to improve. In the midst of this growing sense of life, the idea of one God began to displace the many gods in mankind's awareness.

In the first millennium of this cycle, the people moved and settled in communities with others who shared their beliefs. Warriorship evolved to a finer degree and continued to be a force for good or evil. Scientific curiousity began to express in earnest and gave birth to forms of present day physics, astronomy, biology, chemistry, and mathematics.

Religious thought began to crystalize into a blending of old and new views of Divine relationship and mysticism arose whereby enlightened souls bore witness to their experiences of the Divine reality. Through these witnesses of the truth, man's rituals were often reformed, redefined, and abandoned.

This final 2000 years has seen man's pursuit of truth through science and his pursuit of truth through spirituality.

In this second ascendant cycle of man, all of the elements that were present in the final days of Atlantis are once again present today. It is in this time of transition that the soul of mankind can meet itself, learn the lessons, and be given the opportunity to evolve into closer relationship with the mind of the Divine.

## THE PREPARERS IN THIS TIME OF TRANSITION

Each age of man carries with it a unique learning for the very soul of mankind. And each learning carries with it a need to give a new interpretation of the one Truth and an opportunity to understand and apply this Truth to the body and mind of mankind.

In response to this need, the children of the light would descend from the higher dimensions and take on the challenges of the earthly-framework to aid their brothers and sisters in spirit.

And man's history records the presence of these illuminated souls:

Ra and Hermese, Isis and Osiris in Egypt, Abraham and Moses in the Middle East, Zend and Zoroaster in Persia, Lao-Tze and Confuscius in China, Plato and Socrates in Greece, Krishna and Buddha in India, John the Baptizer and Jesus the Christ in Palestine, Mohammet in the Arabian Lands, Quatzlcoatl in the South American lands.

And there were many, many others in all the races, cultures, and nations of the earth who sought to know and experience the one Truth.

For each of these that were recorded in man's history, there were many children of the light who were often unsung in the chronicles of man. These groups who prepared the way for the coming of the spirit of truth into the earth have been known by many names:

The Expectant Ones, The Remnant, The Elect, The Initiates, The Chosen Ones, The Family of God, The Children of Light, The Brotherhood of the Light, Followers of the Law of One, The Enlightened Ones, The Sons and Daughters of God, The Promised Ones.

And today they are here again to help prepare the way for the re-entrance of the spirit of truth and love into the earth.

This time of transition in which we live is the time wherein all the cycles and the ages of man are coming to an end. All of the characteristics of all the ages are now present in the various systems, regions, races, and cultures that reside on the earth.

The earth itself, is almost bursting with the tremendous number of souls who desire to experience the cleansing, illumination, and the crucible of this present time.

And man's calculations concerning the present times are no longer valid, for time itself is being compressed as the decade of the 90's rushes towards its inevitable conclusion.

In order to assist mankind, the children of the light with those who have prepared themselves for this time, are being asked to embody and bear witness to the spirit of truth and claim all the fruits that this spirit promises to them, and through them, to the very soul of mankind.

## RECOGNIZING THE CHILDREN OF THE LIGHT

The children of the light have been seeded in all walks of earthly life. They reside in all the structures, endeavors, and institutions of man: politically, scientifically, socio-economically, racially, culturally, philosophically, and religiously. Each has been guided and prepared by the spirit of truth for their awakening in this final decade of the millennium.

Within each of this grouping of souls, there is a deep haunting and a sense of purpose and mission that is greater than simple earthly living. Each has a desire to manifest and bear witness to the truth of their personal experiences of the Divine. They seek the truth in all of their endeavors and they persevere in their search, even in the face of obstacles. They possess a deep sense of the oneness of all things in creation. They desire to be made whole again and to form relationships that are supportive and deeply meaningful. They are varied and eclectic in nature, and possess knowledge about the many facets of man's earthly pursuits.

Over the past 30 of the 50 years of this time of transition, many children have felt isolated and alone, misunderstood and alienated from all those others with whom they associate in the earth. They desire to return to their heavenly homes and continually search many paths to find the way to accomplish this.

Many are sensitive and may be prone to environmental illness, both of the earthy-physical and the psychic-mental kind.

Often they are gifted in their creative expressions and are inwardly aware that they possess many more gifts and talents that await the right time to be awakened, expressed, and claimed.

Many are highly intuitive, but often question their own insights in the face of earthly wisdom and opinion. They continually strive to live in accordance with their personally formed principles and have about them, an aura of spiritual nobility. Each has - written in their very heart of hearts - a desire to serve their God, others, and themselves in the very best manner that they can conceive.

The spirit of truth has born witness to all those who seek to give illumination to man, to all those who have lived in accord with their belief and experience of Divine reality, to all those who fought the battle with their earthly natures with courage and peace, and to all those who gave of their lives as a living testimony to their faith.

It is these who are willing to testify with their whole lives who are as the children of the light. It is these who have come in this time to prepare the way for Divine consciousness to repossess the earth. It is these that have come to aid in this Final Crusade.

And it is to these children of the light that we CALL.

## THE AGE OF EXPECTANCY

Today, on the earth, there is a great sense of expectation.

For the sons of earth there is a hope beyond hope that someone or something will intervene and save them from the fate that awaits them on the path of confusion and darkness that they walk. They hope that some scientific breakthrough, some technological innovation, some miraculous solution will materialize in these final hours and point the way out of decay and destruction.

In man's systems of belief, some long for the coming of the messiah or a new prophet for this time. Others await the second coming of the son of God or the Christ. Still others await the spiritual world teacher, the spirit-filled world leader, the reincarnation of avatars, sages, and Divine minds to save mankind from impending oblivion.

To these we say, take heart. The spirit of truth is upon the face of the earth in this very day. It is in all those who call to Him from the four corners of the earth and seek to know and act in accordance with His ways.

But seek first within your own hearts and minds for it is there that He has promised to meet you. Many will say that the spirit of truth resides in some distant land or beside some distant shore. That is not the truth.

For the spirit of truth must first come to the individual, in the body and mind that, through his own choices, may be as a holy temple or a den of iniquity.

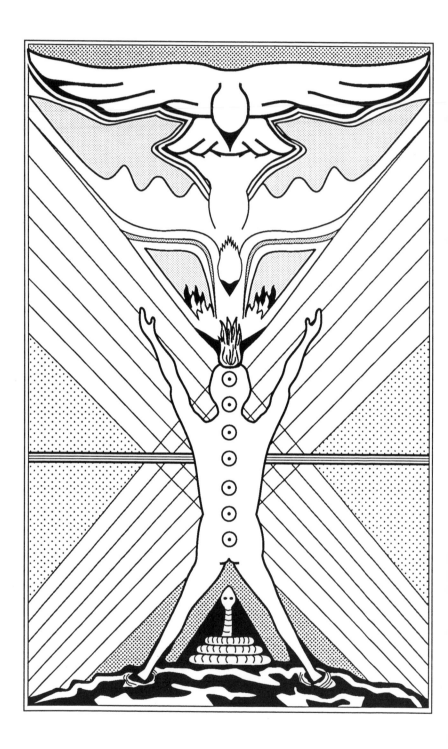

# OUR PERSONAL REVOLUTION

## 2.1 FIRST TO THE INDIVIDUAL

In man's history, all revolutions first begin with an individual. So it is with the spiritual revolution that is washing over the face of the earth at this time...

The CALL comes first to the individual.

This heavenly calling is like a light and a sound that calls to the beings in the higher realms of expression to come and assist the earth in it's impending transformation. As this light and sound descends into the lower vibrational states, it begins to illuminate and to vibrate in the dimensions that correspond to the heart of earth-bound souls.

Within man's heart there resides all of his conscious and unconscious earthly and heavenly desires. All the desires that will lead him towards the light of truth or the darkness of ignorance.

This calling, then, is like an intelligent fire that descends like a dove and inflames these seed-like desires and serves to awaken them. They manifest first as thoughts, imaginings, dreams, visions, and ideas and then, if man has not come to terms with them in the realms of thought, they manifest into an earthly expression.

At the same time, the sexual life force that has been present in man's earthly evolution and lies coiled - like a serpent - at the base of his spine, is awakening and beginning to ascend upward into the heart of man. It too, is like an intelligent fire with eyes that search for and, whose being feeds on, man's deepest desires. It too, will manifest, first in his mind as imagination and then into earthly expression. And it is this earth-bound force - in its essence knowledge without wisdom of the Divine - which has the potential to overcome him.

The fall from earthly grace of religious leaders due to their sexual desires and imbalances is an example of this movement of these two forces in the very being of man. The fall from earthly grace of political leaders who are overcome by their desire for power over men, rather than service to him, is another.

So it is as the prophets have prophecized that the mighty will be made low and the humble in spirit will be raised up in this time of reckoning.

The call for man to awaken to his Divine heritage must then be followed by the cleansing and purging of all his fleshly or earthy desires so that the ascent of the sexual force (serpent) and the descent of the life force (dove) is not impeded.

Then these two seemingly opposed forces can circulate, blend, and become balanced in a type of marriage in ONENESS.

For the children of the light, the strength of this resonance in their hearts will be in direct proportion to their personal desire to seek the truth of their purpose, their mission, and their very existence on the earth.

This spiritual light, sound, or vibration, will inflame and cause their desire to know and experience the Divine to grow and overcome all other desires in their being. And it will be this growing illumination that will guide and lead them through their personal valley of death.

The CALLING, then, is to all souls, but the apprehension and the manifestation of this call will be unique for each individual.

## THE PREPARATIONS FOR THIS TIME

For millennia, the heavens have called to mankind to help awaken him from his state of forgetfulness and to help turn him from his fascination and preoccupation with the things of the earth and return once again to the knowledge of the Divine.

Since the industrial revolution in and around 1860, there began in earnest the preparations for this time of transition. The establishment and the migrations of peoples to centers of commerce and industry, uprooted man's almost exclusive dependence on what was provided directly from the earth. Empires were formed based, not on military might and the need for territory alone, but on an economic interdependence where the resources from one region were transformed in another into products that would serve the needs and desires of man.

Through this development, man was given the opportunity to think, ponder, and explore the mysteries of the earth and the mysteries of his mind. Communication and exploration began to flourish such that there was a blending between the cultures and different understandings of man. There was then a quiet search for a common language by which these different understandings of man could be blended.

The teachings of the east that were founded on an inner exploration of the truth of man's existence on the earth began to intermingle with the teachings of the west in their rationale and scientific and outer explorations of truth.

The great wars advanced the use of technology and science for destruction, but also furthered the ability to aid with those same advancements. Principles, values, and beliefs that supported the old structures began to be more and more reflected upon and questioned.

All was then in readiness for the time of transition that began in the late 1950's and will continue into the early portions of the twenty-first century.

For many, there is an awareness that the past 30 years has been a time of increasing preparation for the testing that will characterize the final decade of the millennium.

The decade of the 60's was a time of preparing the hearts and minds of man, even as a farmer would plough and prepare his fields. The seeds of truth were then planted and took root in the darkness of the 70's. The 80's was a time wherein the truth grew and began to blossom beside the thistles and the weeds of man's old beliefs and habits. And the 90's is a time of choosing, a time of harvesting, and a time of cleansing the heart-fields of man with the fire of creative spirit.

## THE PREPARATIONS IN THE 80'S

The calling of the children of the most high was first felt by many in the period from 1979 to 1981. At that time, there was an initiation and a greater concentration of spiritual energy and information which was funneled onto the earth.

A movement then began within these children to seek for the purpose and truth of their existence and there arose a desire to search for answers to the questions that began to burn within them.

Some answers were found in the existing words of men and the institutions that those men had devised for within all of the creations of earth there resides a portion of that ONE TRUTH. However, the limitations of three-dimensional earthly perception, when acting alone, can never know nor fully experience all of this Divine Truth, but each has the ability to retain and partake in a facet or a portion of that same.

As a consequence, many questions posed by these children remained incompletely and unsatisfactorily answered and there arose a growing sense of personal responsibility for soul growth. This desire for growth led many to begin to explore paths that could yield a deeper understanding of their truth.

Alternative lifestyles, philosophies, and belief systems were pursued, experienced, and then retained for some, as yet unforseen, purpose.

The study of the mystic sciences of astrology, numerology, and geometric shapes and structures were often a portion of their exploration. They studied and cultivated interests in the hidden dimensions of their own minds through psychology, parapsychology, and all forms and manifestations of psychic phenomenon. They probed their distant past through hypnosis, past-life regressions, and channeled readings. They examined the essence of their own spirituality through existing religions, mystery religions, alternate philosophies, and new-thought churches and gatherings. They speculated on the origins of man, from the ancient civilizations of Lemuria and Atlantis to the belief in alien visitations and encounters.

And there were many many more regions and avenues that these children explored.

The result was an acquisition and acceptance of new thoughts, ideas, and beliefs. From 1981 to 1987, many opportunities were availible that allowed these children to experience these new ideas about God, themselves, and their relationship to others.

The calling in the 80's, as in all ages, was deeply personal and unique for that individual. But the awakening to a search for their relationship with the Divine was always preceded by an event that impacted them on some level of their being whether physically, mental-emotionally, or spiritually.

Each event occurred on one or more levels of human awareness and understanding for where one begins his personal search for the truth is where one is in consciousness, physically, mentally, or spiritually.

Whether it was the loss through death of a loved one, the loss of relationship, the loss of acceptance by family and friends, the loss of employment, the loss of self or whether it was the gaining of a vision, the gaining of a dream, the gaining of a still small voice that resonated in the heart, the gaining of insight or intuition or an experience of other dimensions beyond the body...

Each was designed to awaken within the individual a desire to earnestly search for a personal experience of truth.

The legacy that remained with many of the children as they emerged from the 80's was a deep sense of duality. They continued to function in the framework of their old system of beliefs and lifestyles while segregating and nurturing their new system of beliefs into a smaller portion of their earthly life.

They experienced difficulty in integrating spirituality into their homes, social, and work lives. Their feet were planted firmly on the shifting sands of the old-system while their hearts yearned for the coming of an opportunity to express the new-system they had experienced.

Then came the calling in August of 1987 that was a convergence of the heavenly bodies and spheres in harmony and in response to the desires of the children who strove to be of the light.

## THE CALLING FROM 1987 TO THE PRESENT

The calling in 1987 was like a pebble that was dropped from the etheric realms into the very hearts of these children. The ripples and waves of change that emanate from this descent of the spirit will allow them the opportunity to transform themselves, in co-operation with the Divine, in body, mind, and soul.

In response, a new movement began to manifest and a new type of awakening began to flow into their conscious awareness.

Before their descent into the earth, the children of the light who had chosen to incarnate since 1929, reaffirmed their original covenant with the Divine and with the earth. This covenant, which resides within and is written on their very hearts, is to aid in awakening their brother and sister souls to the light and the love of the Divine.

The call in 1987, then, was a call to activate and stimulate a conscious awareness of the presence of this Divine covenant.

The movement, prompted by the resonance and the urgings of their hearts, was then to seek out and to reach out to those souls who may have become mired in the mundane issues of the earth. These awakened ones may have been consciously unaware of the purpose in this movement, but despite their lack of fuller understanding, they continued to move to form new relationships with family, society, and their working environments.

Those who were, in a sense, more awakened to their mission and soul's purpose, were sent to those less awakened in order to teach and to aid. This occurred through situations, groups, books, readings, crisis, and trauma. This movement in relationship has and does continue to occur throughout this time of transition.

From January 15th to April 15th of 1991, a great division occurred in the consciousness of man. Those few months were a time of choosing whether to awaken and honour the light of the Divine or to honour the darkness. Each soul on the earth was tested and was affected in some way.

For the children of the light and all those who had prepared and had, to that point, continually chosen the light, it was a time of deciding how much farther they would allow their emerging awareness of soul's mission - and the transformed earthly role that it would bring with it - to impact their present earthly lives. It was a time of choosing whether to more fully respond to the call to the Final Crusade, or to continue in a semblance of their past earthly lifestyle.

For this time of transition is a time of sifting. It is a time of separation between the words of light and those of darkness. It is a time of re-examining the beliefs in life and love from those that were blended over time with fear and death.

But where the threshing and the sifting must first occur is within.

For those who have prepared themselves through meditation, prayer, and self-study and have acted in such a way as to find approval in their own eyes and in the eyes of the God that they worship, this call was and will continue to be felt with an impacting knowingness. In this time, as each individual asks the heavens for greater understanding and awareness, Divine wisdom, confirmation, and validation will be given to help guide each to discern the truth.

But the first step is to KNOW THYSELF.

For it is within, by your seeking to know yourself and your relationship to the heavens, that you will come to find the truth of your earthly existence.

## 2.2 THE CALL TO KNOW YOURSELF

In the beginning, the seven Divine rays emanated from the First Cause and, by the blending of this creative light with the all-knowing darkness, began the process of shaping and forming the earthly-framework.

Each ray or vibration held the pattern of its own unfoldment and was aware of the seed within the seed that was contained within it.

First there came the gases, then the molten minerals, then the land and the waters, then the plants and vegetation, then the fish and all manner of creatures of the seas, the fowl and the birds of the air, and the beasts and animals that walked upon the face of the earth.

Each, in their turn, held sway over the earth and each could be likened to an earthly kingdom.

The sixth vibration, more complex than it's five predecessors, combined with all the previous earthly elements to form a new expression of the Divine that would be known as the sons of earth or the sons of man.

The seventh ray or vibration was - in it's essence - Divine consciousness and was embodied by that group of souls that would be known as the children of the light or the sons of God.

In order, however, to allow the sons of earth access to the Divine consciousness as embodied by the sons of God, the body of man was altered to accommodate this new awareness. As a result, in the legends, myths, and scriptures of man's knowledge, there resides the concept of the original or primordial earthly parents.

There were five expressions of these new human forms that occurred simultaneously on the earth about 25,000 years ago, each corresponding to the five races of man:

The white race expressed as Adam and Eve in that region of the earth known as Mesopotamia. The red race expressed as Atlas and Mauri in that legendary continent known as Atlantis. The yellow race expressed as Mu and Cho-ephra in that land known today as southern China near Siam. The brown race expressed as Maya and Sanu in ancient Lemuria, which in this day would be as the west coast of South America. And the black race expressed as Ashanti and Vsni in the very heart of that land known as Africa.

These altered forms of earthly human expression took root in the earth and multiplied and were the means through which the sons of God could commune and associate with the sons of the earth. They walked and shared and communed in karmic and spiritual relationships on the first ascendant cycle of mankind.

The destruction of Atlantis caused a tremendous movement of the earthly waters and thus arose, in man's remembrance, the legends and the myths of the Great Flood.

Those souls who were sufficiently quickened and attuned to hear the call of the heavens in that time, worked to preserve themselves, their families, and their goods with the purpose of repopulating the earth after this great purge or cleansing.

Those others who had chosen the mundane and had attuned themselves to the things of the earth were unaware of the approaching cataclysms and continued to buy and sell, barter and trade, and act in accordance with their old ways until they perished in the midst of their chosen ignorance.

It is, and has always been, the Creator's desire that man awaken to his Divine nature. But it is man's choice as to what and to whom he will attune his awareness. It is the Creator's promise that in each circumstance, situation, or event that confronts mankind in the earthly-frame-work, there is provided a way and a means of escaping into Divine awareness.

The sign or symbol of this covenant or Divine promise with mankind, is the rainbow that can be seen in the heavens in the aftermath of a storm.

And the path, the bridge, the way of escape, can be found within the very body and nature of man, himself.

## REFLECTIONS ON THE SOUL

For thousands of years, man has speculated on the origins, presence, and nature of the soul. How was it that something immaterial in form and idea could have relationship with him in the earth? If the idea of a soul was true, how could it interact and communicate with the body and mind of man and where within would it choose to reside?

Before the beginning, with the intent of souls to descend (whether from the sixth or the seventh vibrations) into the lower states of awareness and physicality on the earthly-framework, there was an understanding in the heavens that the connection with the Divine must some-how be maintained.

The Divine's response to this understanding was to place the means for man to connect with his soul at any level of belief or existence. In turn, the Divine furnished the way for the soul of man to meet, interact, and communicate with any level of man's being as he expresses in the earth.

The wonder of God's expression in the earth, His wisdom and His majesty, can be found within the speck of Divine intent that is known as the soul.

Within each soul, there is remembrance of all things and the harmony of relationship to the First Cause. There is a memory of gazing upon and participating in the song of creation with love and with rapture. And there is the feeling of wonder and awe at the magnificence of the mind of that Great and Universal Being.

Within each soul, there is the ability to discern, remember, and comprehend the truth. There resides the ability for illumination and with that same, the potential for creatively redefining that truth. And there is the spark of life that allows this truth and illumination to be made manifest and, in this way, bring healing for self and for others.

The difficulty that was felt before the beginning, was how the Divine light of the soul should be imbedded within the physical nature of man. How could the connection with the Divine remain and still allow an expression and experience of physicality in the earth? How could this experiment in free-will, where man could choose to dwell in the earth alone or evolve to be a dweller in the heavens while on the earth, be truly and faithfully enacted?

Thus, it was determined by that great mind, that to fulfill all these desires, the energy or vibration of the soul was separated and differentiated into the seven centers or chakras that are the meeting places of the soul within the physical body of man.

These seven centers are reflections of the seven rays that formed the earthly framework and form joints, junctures, or connections with the nervous systems of man.

And the presence of these centers of communion are the fulfillment of the Divine covenant that no soul shall ever be forgotten.

## THE SEVEN CENTERS OR RAYS IN THE BODY OF MAN

The lowest vibration or awareness, which most closely aligns with man's physical expression, was placed in the first center or chakra. This same differentiation placed the highest awareness, which most closely aligns with man's spiritual expression, into the seventh center or chakra.

Between these two was placed a veil of forgetfulness which resides in the very heart of man. The soul, then, would awaken first to its physical nature in the earth and then could choose to further re-awaken, through these centers, to its spiritual nature in the course of its earthly existence.

Whatever center or group of centers opens and begins to function becomes, in essence, the seat or place of residence of the soul within man.

The _**first chakra**_, or the Gonad center, can be called the gravity chakra for it is found to be in closest relationship to the earth. This center serves to draw the individual to

## IMAGE: THE SEVEN DIVINE RAYS & THEIR EARTHLY ASSOCIATIONS

| RAY CENTER | GLAND (Nerve System) | ELEMENT (Planet) | SOUND (Instrument) | COLOUR | SPIRIT (Law) | IMAGE (Crystal) |
|---|---|---|---|---|---|---|
| 7 | PINEAL — Crown Of Head | AUM — Aman | TEE — Silence | INDIGO | ILLUMINATION — Oneness | ENCIRCLED DOVE — Rose Quartz |
| 6 | PITUITARY — Base Of Brain | LIGHT — Neptune | LA — Harp | VIOLET | TRUTH — Truth | SUN — Blue Amethyst |
| 5 | THYROID — Cervical | ETHER — Pluto | SO — Pan Flute | BLUE | WILL — Desire | FIRE of the HOLY SPIRIT — Emerald/Blue Sapphire |
| 4 | THYMUS — Dorsal | AIR — Venus | FA — Flute | GREEN | EARTHLY LOVE — Harmony | HEART — Diamond/Ruby |
| 3 | ADRENAL — Lumbar | FIRE — Earth | ME — Brass | YELLOW | PRESERVATION — Cause & Effect | PYRAMID — Topaz |
| 2 | LYDEN — Sacral | WATER — Mercury | RAY — Bass | ORANGE | REPRODUCTION — Creativity | LOVERS — Tigers Eye |
| 1 | GONADS — Coccyx | EARTH — Mars | DOE — Drum | RED | GRAVITY — Life | IRON — Red Sapphire |

HEAVENLY (rays 7, 6, 5, 4)

EARTHLY (rays 4, 3, 2, 1)

## IMAGE: THE SEVEN RAYS in the BODY of MAN

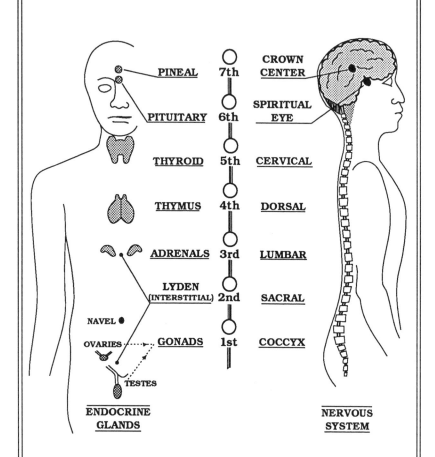

| ENDOCRINE GLANDS | | NERVOUS SYSTEM |
|---|---|---|
| PINEAL | 7th | CROWN CENTER |
| PITUITARY | 6th | SPIRITUAL EYE |
| THYROID | 5th | CERVICAL |
| THYMUS | 4th | DORSAL |
| ADRENALS | 3rd | LUMBAR |
| LYDEN (INTERSTITIAL) | 2nd | SACRAL |
| GONADS | 1st | COCCYX |

NAVEL
OVARIES
TESTES

THE SEVEN CENTERS ARE THE JUNCTURES WITHIN THE
NERVOUS SYSTEM OF MAN THAT ALLOWS CONNECTIONS
WITH MAN'S SOUL. THROUGH THESE CENTERS THERE IS
THE FULFILLMENT OF THE DIVINE PROMISE THAT
NO SOUL SHALL EVER BE FORGOTTEN.

the core of the earth just as the seventh center seeks to draw the soul of man to the very core of the Divine.

Through this first center, the soul feels the necessities and ways of being and living in the earth most clearly, for it is the place where man first becomes aware of the purpose and understanding of his physical nature.

It is the center where the soul is grounded and works with the soils, waters, and animals of the earth in expressions and understandings of the physical or natural laws that comprise the earthly framework. The emotions that originate and are felt by this center, are fear and anger with the things, circumstances, and limitations that man's soul must face while in the earth.

The **_second chakra_** is the Lyden center which retains the purpose of man's reproduction in the earth. It is the center that influences the fertility and sexuality within man, and concerns itself with relationships that are earthy and physical in nature.

This second center vibrates in harmony with the first chakra and serves to blend and harmonize between the gonads and the adrenals. In this way, it can be called the mind of the body and the residence and source of man's conscious awareness.

The Divine promise contained within this second center is man's ability to reproduce himself and to creatively manifest in the earth. The aspect of the soul's memory that acts through this center is that which pertains to reproduction or like begetting like and the memory of how to survive in the earth. This instinct, or will for survival, impels man to fight for his continued earthly existence and for those children or offspring who he has created.

This center is a higher awareness or vibration than the first chakra, for it serves to move man from a pre-occupation with self in earthly relationship alone, towards a higher and broader awareness of others in relationship to his earthly purpose.

The **_third chakra_** is the Adrenal center or solar plexus which retains and contains the spirit or purpose of the preservation of self. It is the karmic mind of the body and retains the memories of all the soul's incarnations, manifestations, relationships, and interrelationships in the earth.

This third center can be called the power center in the body of man, for by focusing attention on this chakra, the physical body of man can be greatly augmented and strengthened. It provides the energy or emotions that stand behind the thoughts of man and contains the courage and determination to persevere in manifesting those thoughts.

The adrenals are associated with the diaphram and digestive systems such that the rate and depth of breathing can affect this gland. When man cannot digest or stomach the experience that enters his conscious awareness, all the organs associated with the physical digestive process are adversely affected.

As a repository of karmic memory, it retains all the deeds and misdeeds of man's sojourns, and through fear, guilt, and self-doubt, is the center that is most often misdirected.

Through the solar-plexus, man can project himself beyond the physical shell and obtain information and experiences in the lower realms of vibration. In this way, man can sense the spirit, power, or emotions from others in the earth.

Of all man's centers, this center poses the greatest potential barrier to the conscious movement of information rising towards the spiritual nature and soul awareness of man. In turn, the solar-plexus acts as a barrier to the soul's knowledge and information descending into man's conscious awareness.

The *fourth chakra*, Thymus, or heart center has the purpose of expressing the love of Divine and the love of man in the earth. It is as a bridge between man's earthly and spiritual natures, and in many ways, is the most important center in man.

This chakra is the crossroads and interplays with the body, mind, and soul of man. It is the storehouse organ for all the other centers for it impacts the circulatory and respiratory systems that maintain life within the body of man.

Just as the lyden can be equated with the logical, analytical, and rational conscious mind of man, the thymus can be equated with the unconscious mind of man.

The heart center is the vibration or dimension that is most often used by the etheric or heavenly realms to communicate and aid in the healing of the individual.

This fourth center may act as a bridge or a barrier to man's evolution, for it is the center that is most often shrouded in grayness and cloudiness. For when the love within man has been misguided, misdirected, or misused, there is a pain, numbness, and an inability for the heart to function properly.

There is a tremendous pressure on this center (due to its interplay with all the aspects of man) to keep the bodily and mental functions in some sense of cohesive awareness. The heart has the ability to sense the lower and the higher emotions and is often caught in the duality of man's two-fold nature.

Thus, the opening or awakening of these three or four lower centers define the physical or earthly expression of man's soul.

When man focuses his attention on physicality, he can be bonded to the earth. He will be able to reproduce himself. He will be able to deal with karmic memory (even though this dealing may be on an unconscious level). And he will be able to experience some stirrings of his heart.

From man's perspective, the individual can be considered to be performing and functioning well in the earth.

For those whose earthly life progresses with no further thought of love or of the Divine, the heart and the higher spiritual centers will begin to degenerate over time. That individual is said to become hard-hearted, stiff-necked, and hard-headed in his relationship with self and others. As this hardened shell of beliefs, thoughts, and feelings solidifies, it is more and more difficult for that individual to begin the path of spiritual awakening.

However, when the individual begins to earnestly desire an alignment with the Divine intent within him, there is a stirring of his soul and the beginning of the opening of the remaining higher or spiritual chakras.

The *fifth chakra*, Thyroid center, or throat chakra is the center that defines the will or very life of the soul. It contains within it the ability to understand that, for

Divine alignment to occur, the soul's own will and desires must guide and direct the individual. The clamoring and thundering of the lower vibrational centers must give way to the still small voice of the Divine that ever resonates within.

This fifth center is most often blocked or closed in man. The effects of this closure can manifest as difficulties in the eyes, ears, nose, throat, mouth, jaws, and even the teeth. All areas from the base of the neck to the eyebrows of the head can be adversely affected.

However, when this center begins to open, there is experienced a gradual clearing in the throat, ears, and sinus passages accompanied by a tremendous confusion. The confusion arises by the efforts of this center to re-align the soul within the body of man and the inability of the individual to release the inharmonious memories of his earthly sojourns. The inability to express, verbalize, communicate or let go of his emergent thoughts and feelings leads him to experience great confusion.

The opening of this center initiates and precipitates the struggle between man's spiritual and his earthly natures. The battleground becomes the heart, mind, and body where the love of man and the love of the Divine can intermingle and commune.

The **_sixth chakra_** or Pituitary center is the spiritual eye within the body of man. The Divine promise embodied by this center is that each and every soul can express in ways that are creative. The opening of this center allows the flow of information, inspiration, and intuition to man's conscious awareness. Through this center, the soul of man may project itself and explore other dimensions and states of awareness, but in a limited way.

The pituitary is the master gland of the body. As it begins to open, it harmonizes, attunes, and cleanses the lower chakras and centers.

Through visions and images received by this spiritual eye, it apprehends the light of the Divine and circulates and shares this light with the entire body and mind of man. For if the purpose of man is singular and one with Divine intent, man's whole body will be filled with light.

Just as the lyden is the conscious mind and the thymus is the unconscious mind, the pituitary houses the cosmic, super, or soul-mind consciousness within the body of man.

The SOURCE of this cosmic or super-conscious perception of the oneness and love of the Divine is the seventh center or crown chakra.

Between the spritual eye and the crown chakra, there is an intimate relationship. As the spiritual eye begins to open, its vibrations begin to resonate in harmony with the crown chakra. In response, the crown chakra begins to open and resonates back and further stimulates the spiritual eye.

The spiritual eye or pituitary contains the soul's ability to apprehend the truth of the Divine. The crown chakra or pineal, however, contains the ability to comprehend the illumination of the Divine that allows a co-creative reshaping and redefining of this truth.

For the body of man to be prepared to receive the enlightenment that would flow to it from his crown or highest center, the spiritual eye must first be awakened to cleanse the memories and toxins within the genetic memories, body cells, and soul memories. In this way, the body is prepared to accept the gifts of the spirit that the opening of the seventh seal would bring.

The **_seventh chakra_**, Pineal, or crown center is the ability by the soul to experience the knowledge and the oneness with the Divine.

As the first chakra connects man to the core of the earth, the seventh chakra connects man to the core of the First Cause.

Although the soul may leave the body through the solar plexus or the spiritual eye, the way the soul should ever strive to leave the physical body of man is through the crown chakra.

When the soul leaves through this seventh center, it has the ability to project itself into all the realms and dimensions of the universes without limitation. It can see, hear, feel, and experience those realms in clairaudient, clairvoyant, and clairsentient ways. It has access to all the corners and recesses of the mind of the Divine. It has the ability to receive illumination, to experience visions, and to be ONE with all that is. It will remember from the very foundations of creation and the beginning of time and be able to project into the future of all times. And it will be able to commune with the angels, saints, prophets, and most holy men and women, and with the Holy of Holies and the Creator of all things.

The opening of the seventh chakra is the way to illumination and enlightenment for the body, mind, and soul of mankind. And by and through its awakening, the seven are merged again into one.

## PHYSICAL AND SPIRITUAL SOUL AWAKENINGS

When man first became aware that he was man and walked the face of the earth over one million years ago, there was the body physical with all its attributes and there was the body mental with its ability to reason and analyse.

The physical body adhered to the natural laws and required the sustenance that the earth could provide. The mental body was needed to support the physical needs of the body in terms of food, shelter, warmth, and the fight for survival against nature and the beasts that then roamed the earth.

As man evolved, the third level of emotions and karmic memories of earthly sojourns began to emerge and there was a blending of the body and mind of man through the expression of these emotions. In this way, the body was given more credence by the mind and the emotions evolved into greater and greater importance in man's earthly development.

As the emergence of man's emotional nature and the inherent power contained within this nature was felt, the body, mind, and soul of man were all profoundly affected.

The soul would utilize the emotions to cause man to feel joy, inspiration, and creativity. The soul would use the emotions to warn man of impending danger, to give man a feeling of uneasiness in incorrect situations, or to alert man to the fact that he may be mislead by the words and the actions of others.

At the same time, the body and the mind of man would also interplay with the emotions. So often, this interplay would result in doubt, worry, fear, pride, and ego of the

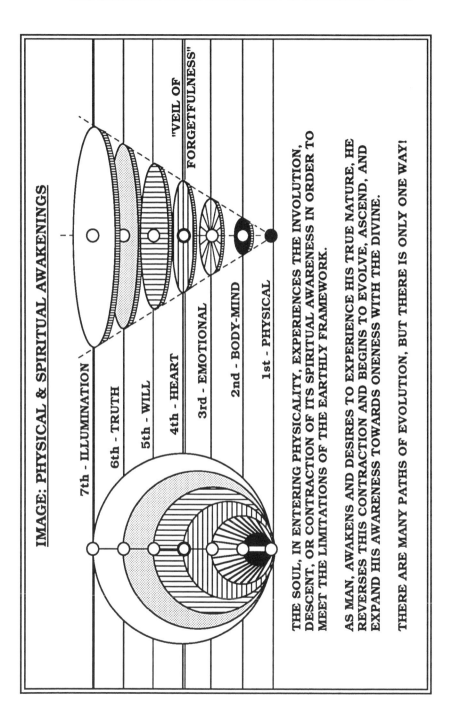

IMAGE: PHYSICAL & SPIRITUAL AWAKENINGS

7th - ILLUMINATION

6th - TRUTH

5th - WILL

4th - HEART

3rd - EMOTIONAL

2nd - BODY-MIND

1st - PHYSICAL

"VEIL OF FORGETFULNESS"

THE SOUL, IN ENTERING PHYSICALITY, EXPERIENCES THE INVOLUTION, DESCENT, OR CONTRACTION OF ITS SPIRITUAL AWARENESS IN ORDER TO MEET THE LIMITATIONS OF THE EARTHLY FRAMEWORK.

AS MAN, AWAKENS AND DESIRES TO EXPERIENCE HIS TRUE NATURE, HE REVERSES THIS CONTRACTION AND BEGINS TO EVOLVE, ASCEND, AND EXPAND HIS AWARENESS TOWARDS ONENESS WITH THE DIVINE.

THERE ARE MANY PATHS OF EVOLUTION, BUT THERE IS ONLY ONE WAY!

mind. The physical response to these negative mental and emotional states would yield a pain in the heart that would cause a stroke or an attack or the inability of the body to release or eliminate doubt, worry, and anxiety would impact the kidneys and the liver.

The soul, then, uses the emotions. The mind and body of man also uses the emotions, and the result of this dual and diverse interplay is often havoc, confusion, and the lack of understanding and evolvement of the consciousness within man.

This was the "state" that existed in the soul of mankind when the seventh vibration was sent by the Divine into the earthly-framework nearly 100 thousand years ago. And this is the "state" of body and mind that man so often finds within himself in this present day.

The call from the heavens, then, is not to awaken man to his physical, emotional, or mental nature, but rather for man to awaken to his spiritual nature.

## Physical Awakening in the Soul of Man

When conception occurs in the earth, it is seen in the heavens as a light or a beacon that beckons and signals to all souls the opportunity for physical manifestation. This light draws those aligned souls who are ready for evolvement through those particular learnings and purposes.

One soul, in a sense, chooses and is chosen, and begins to explore the environs, minds, and psyches of those who would care for this new-born in the earth. When appropriate, this soul descends further, begins to dim its awareness through the veil of forgetfulness, and assumes the garments and challenges of the flesh.

The first center in the body of man that awakens to the soul's physical existence is the heart center. For it is not just circulation and respiration that is required to maintain the spark of life within the body, but it is this newborn's need for the sustenance given by love. The presence of love strengthens the soul's connection to the body. The absence of love weakens this connection. And the highest expression of love in the earth can be found in the experience of a mother's love for a child.

The second center that normally awakens is the gonads or the first chakra, for this is the center that roots or imbeds the soul within the body. There is usually time needed by the soul to become accustomed to the confines and limitations of the body and, as a result, this center is not fully open, nor is the soul fully embedded, for many weeks after the soul's physical entrance into the earthly-framework.

The third center that normally awakens in the earth is the adrenals. Here the individual begins to deal with karmic memories and accesses information from the lower vibrational states for the learning of the soul. Often this center will not fully open until the age of three or four years.

The fourth and final earthly center to awaken is the Lyden where the conscious awareness of the body becomes activated with the maturation of the sexual and reproductive organs during that phase of development known as puberty.

When there arises in the individual a desire for further illumination of his being, a different kind of awakening overcomes him. Through that desire, the individual begins to give credence to the presence and existence of his soul and, as a consequence, that soul becomes empowered and begins to reawaken the chakras to their Divine intent.

In this way, there is an experience in the body and mind of man of being reborn, not in the earth, but in and of the spirit.

## Spiritual Awakenings in the Body of Man

The frustration for those who begin to take responsibility for their spiritual understanding, attunement, and alignment with the Divine, is the overshadowing by the lower vibrations of physicality of the higher vibrations of their spiritual natures.

The individual who seeks oneness with the Divine, must make an effort to go beyond the familiar sense of his body and his earthly mind. He must make an effort to contemplate the Divine reality, focus his attention on the heavens, and desire to seek and act in accordance with light and truth.

Then his soul will move to whatever level of awareness and understanding is needed to meet and aid that individual in his spiritual ascent.

As that individual continues and perseveres in re-claiming personal responsibility for spiritual growth, there begins to emerge a deeper understanding of the universal power of love.

For all spiritual awakening has its beginnings and its endings in love. It is love that impels and compels man to move beyond the bindings of the three lower chakras and, in response to this emergent awareness of love, the soul quickens and causes a further awakening in the body and the mind of the individual and his heart chakra begins to open.

Blended within the heart of man is the love of self, the love of others, and the love of the Divine. So often man becomes entrapped and delayed in his spiritual ascent because he cannot move beyond this love of self and the love of others in intimate earthly relationships.

So often forgotten in the midst of man's spiritual awakening in the earth is the love of the Divine.

The soul leads man into spiritual awakening through the power of love. On the soul's journey in the earth, there must arise an understanding and a feeling of love for self and others. But what is often mislaid is the knowledge that each earthly relationship, either with self or with others, is a reflection or a preparation for the experience of love Divine.

For how could the love of the Divine flow into the conscious awareness of the individual if that individual had never experienced a natural love in the earth?.

What must be remembered, then, is the love of the Divine, the love of seeking and experiencing the truth, and the love for love's sake alone.

When man comes to this understanding, he moves beyond the love in the earth, and the three spiritual centers begin to awaken.

The first spiritual center to awaken is the fifth or throat chakra. Through this fifth dimensional awareness, the ancient battle in the heavens between the spirit of truth (soul-will) and the spirit of error is re-enacted within the body and mind of the individual.

What initially impacts man's awareness in attuning and opening his higher spiritual centers is intense turmoil, struggle, and confusion.

The throat chakra's awakening can cause the heart center to, in a sense, erupt from the hurt, pain, and suppressed thoughts and emotions the individual harboured. In this emotional releasing, a whirlwind of thoughts and images can billow and froth into man's conscious awareness.

The karmic memories with all their associated emotions that served as a barrier to the ascent and descent of energy and information, will begin to break down and flood, in almost overwhelming waves of re-experiencing, into his conscious awareness.

The fear of the loss of self emerges and the earthly expressions of that individual will begin to change dramatically. For the fight within the individual is the struggle between his spiritual and earthly intent, between the will and desires of his soul and the will and desires of his body and mind, and between the expression of love as selflessness and the earthly power of selfishness.

If the true purpose and desire for walking the spiritual path is for earthly power in the material realms or psychic-mental power in the spiritual realms, then the individual will be prevented from advancing further by his own soul. For the soul, rather than incurring upon itself further error, will disallow the personality, ego, or body-mind from further progress on the path while holding a power-seeking intent.

To enter the heavenly realms, man's pride and self-aggrandizement must be released. Self-interest must be sacrificed for the sake of Divine-interest. For the greatest amongst men are those who desire to serve the Divine and mankind with the humility and selflessness that is found in loving for love's sake alone.

When this battle is done and there is an understanding of humility, the soul-will leads the mind and body of the individual to a further ascent toward the sixth and seventh chakras.

The resonance of the fifth center serves to awaken the sixth center or spiritual eye and there is a corresponding impact and stimulation, cleansing, harmonizing, and quickening of all of the centers within man.

As the seventh chakra or Christ consciousness is awakened through the self-work and preparation of the individual in accordance with his understanding of love Divine, all the vibrations of all the other centers are further raised and quickened. As well as the ascent of life into love, there is a simultaneous descent of Divine love into man's earthly life that flushes with a cleansing and illuminating intent, in a coiling and serpentine manner, upwards and downwards, in waves of joy and harmony.

Within and through this way, there is a re-unification, blending, and marriage of the spiritual and earthly natures of man.

### The Ascent of the Energies within Man

Throughout the path of spiritual awakening, there is an evolution or movement of energy that rises from the base, root, or first chakra ever upwards towards the mind of the Divine. In eastern thought, this movement is termed kundalini and is imaged as a serpent that seeks to mate with the wisdom of the Divine.

On the spiritual path, there are experienced many degrees of awakenings, cleansings, or kundalinis which may be subtle or impacting.

The gentle or subtle kundalinis occur each time the individual directs his awareness or moves in accordance with his image of the Divine. Actual creation, transmutation, and transformation occurs and re-occurs within the body and mind of the seeker. Remember always, no effort to seek the truth and to reclaim one's Divine heritage is for naught, even though the seeker may be unaware of the changes and the progress that is occurring within him.

Others who have allowed more profound and impacting movements of this Divine and earthly energy, experience a change that affects their very metabolism, the DNA factor, genetic memory, and results in a purging of toxins from their physical, mental, and emotional natures that act as deterrants to spiritual remembrance, learning, and illumination.

When there is a full kundalini wherein the individual knows he has been struck by the power of God, received a miraculous vision, or experienced one or more levels of spiritual reality or healing, then what has occurred is that the individual - in consort with his soul - has allowed all his seven centers to be stimulated by the power and the energy of love.

Then there follows a complete transformation and the ability for spiritual emergence into the earthly framework in unique and unexpected ways.

## THE SEVEN ROADS TO REMEMBRANCE

As each soul descends into earthly incarnation, it passes through a veil of forgetfulness that was placed by the Divine to allow the drama and experiment of personal or free will to be enacted on the earth.

Each soul that passes through this veil chooses to incarnate for a specific purpose and a specific learning. And until the learning is completed, the knowledge of the soul's mission cannot fully enter conscious awareness.

Through his seven centers, man has the ability to access all of his personal and soul memories. All of his experiences, thoughts, feelings, desires, learnings and purposes are recorded within his soul and within the mind of the Divine. Each soul has a place and a record within God's book of remembrance and even though man may forget his relationship with the Divine, the Divine ever remembers His relationship to man.

To penetrate this veil of forgetfulness and read the record of his soul's manifestations, man must strive to focus and attune the purpose and desire of his body, mind, and heart to the mind of the Divine.

In this way, the calling that resonates within the minds of men, may serve - if he so chooses - to bring all things back to his awareness from the very foundations of the earth and from the very beginnings of time.

For there is only one time, one space, one source, and one mind. That one and great light divided itself into seven lesser lights which are embodied in the seven centers of man. Through man's choices, through the awakening of the lights of his body, he may become fully aware of his co-creative relationship to the Divine or seek to create for himself and others, a virtual hell upon the earthly-framework.

For be aware that the all-knowing darkness that existed and still exists in the universes is not the same as the darkness of ignorance that has been created and fed by the selfish purposes, the spirit of rebellion, and the fear filled falsehoods that reside in the limited thinking and beliefs of mankind.

In each lifetime, within each incarnation, each soul has been called more than once by the Divine. And it is in ignorance that the call has been suppressed and unacknowledged. Today, there is yet another opportunity and another call to allow the light of truth to overcome the darkness of ignorance that weighs heavily upon man's soul.

It is for each individual to prepare himself and attune the ears of his awareness to hear the call of the Divine. Once heard, it is for each individual to choose how and with what purpose he will respond.

The seven centers within the body of man are as gatherings or focal points of common purpose. If all are aligned to one purpose and the seven eyes and seven ears within these centers are attuned to listen and gaze upon the love of the Divine, man's whole body will be filled with light.

Then, through the lighting of the seven lamps of his body, man will be offered the means by which he may refashion himself into a noble and glorified earthly expression of his Image of God.

## 2.3  OUR IMAGE OF GOD

It has been written that man was made in the image of God and since the dawn of recorded history, he has pondered and reflected in an effort to gain insight and understanding of this phrase.

For those who interpret this phrase literally, their image of God is as a body or an expression in human or earthly forms. The Great One is seen by these as an old white haired and bearded man who sits upon a throne in the far and distant Kingdom of Heaven. He manifests into the earth as a god of law, a law that is rigid, inflexible, and yet, somehow - and often incomprehensibly - just in his pronouncements.

There is a fear that is nurtured and maintained by those who worship this god that is sustained by man's ignorance of his own condition. This god comes to earth infrequently, for if god is good, why would he associate with a world and a people that are - in their very essence - evil? But when he does come, he comes in retribution and punishment for all the evil men have done and continue to do to this very day.

Those who are as the philosophers, theologians, and thinkers strive to look beyond the literal interpretation of the image of God and focus their attention on the thought or meaning behind it.

They view their god as a great mind that wove the idea of the universes from his imagination or his dreams. The earth, with all its multitude of forms and expressions, is simply the product of this one great mind. They view their god as one that is based on belief and desire. They subscribe to a doctrine that, by simply understanding and applying the laws which govern the mind, they will obtain dominion over the earth and all its multitude of expressions. To these, god may be present or may be absent from their day-to-day earthly life, dependent on their beliefs.

But this god is a god of duality, for the mind of man is dual by its very nature. Dependent on the attitude that is held, their Image of God can bring illumination and clarity, or darkness and confusion into their earthly experience.

For there is never one as confused as one who truly believes he sees all clearly.

Then there are those mystics and enlightened ones who look beyond the form and the meaning of the Image of God and strive to see the purpose and the intent that stands behind it.

They view their god as spirit, light, energy, and love. They possess an inner awareness that the spirit which underlies the action is more important than the meaning or the form that the action may become.

There is an unchanging and unerring sameness about their god, for they feel that the spirit is the fabric that binds all meaning and manifestation together and is the place in which these two reside.

And they know, through their personal experiences, that this spirit is the all-knowing and true and ever-present nature of the Divine. What makes this spirit of the Divine a Holy Spirit in the earth, is man's awakening to a conscious awareness of its existence.

It was not, then, man's earthly expression that was

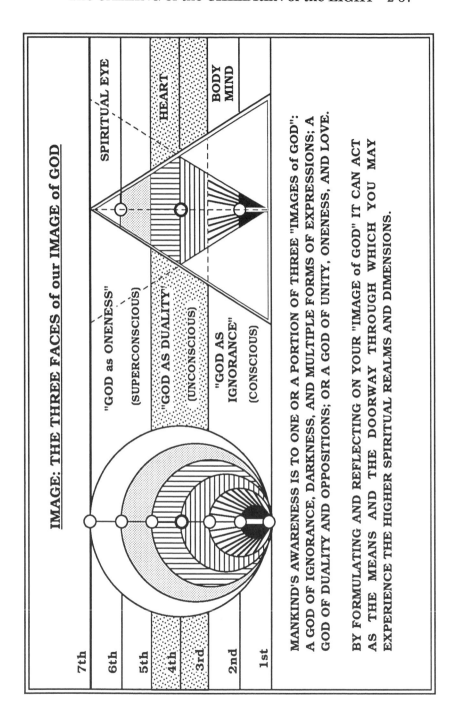

IMAGE: THE THREE FACES of our IMAGE of GOD

SPIRITUAL EYE

HEART

BODY
MIND

"GOD as ONENESS"
(SUPERCONSCIOUS)

"GOD AS DUALITY"
(UNCONSCIOUS)

"GOD AS
IGNORANCE"
(CONSCIOUS)

7th
6th
5th
4th
3rd
2nd
1st

MANKIND'S AWARENESS IS TO ONE OR A PORTION OF THREE "IMAGES of GOD":
A GOD OF IGNORANCE, DARKNESS, AND MULTIPLE FORMS OF EXPRESSIONS; A
GOD OF DUALITY AND OPPOSITIONS; OR A GOD OF UNITY, ONENESS, AND LOVE.

BY FORMULATING AND REFLECTING ON YOUR "IMAGE of GOD" IT CAN ACT
AS THE MEANS AND THE DOORWAY THROUGH WHICH YOU MAY
EXPERIENCE THE HIGHER SPIRITUAL REALMS AND DIMENSIONS.

formed in the image of God, but rather his spiritual or soul expression.

## THE MANY GODS OF MANKIND

To grow in understanding of the many gods that man worships, one needs to only observe where it is that man focuses and places his attention. For wherever man places and focuses his attention, there will be his god.

To some in the earth, their god is a god of materialism whereby the acquisition of the fruits of the earth, and the temporal pleasures that these fruits can bring, become their primary motivations. Wealth, sexual gratification, and intoxication are all the goals of their obsessive search for earthly power and pleasure and are the means by which they measure their success.

They often subscribe to a hedonistic or humanistic philosophy and - if a higher power or god exists in their belief structures - this god does not involve himself in day-to-day earthly existence, but is transcendent and only exists for them in some other dimension of time and space.

The system and earthly structures in which these individuals participate and devise, are often self-serving and they continually try to control and manipulate them to make them ever more so.

Others worship a god of technology wherein their faith is placed in man's ingenuity, resourcefulness, and inventiveness, often to the exclusion of the Divine.

Science and technology, in and of themselves, are not evil. But how man determines to apply these same will yield either a helpful or a hurtful influence in his life and in the lives of those around him. Be assured that man, acting on his own, can create nothing of lasting value, for he merely shapes and rearranges what already exists. But man, in co-operation with the Divine, can participate in the creation and evolution of the universe itself.

Still others worship a god of institutions whereby the political, economic, religious, business, and social structures become the areas where these have placed their faith.

This search by man for a higher power has lead him in error to the power of the people as in the realms of politics; the power of money as in the banking, financial, and other economic structures; the power of beliefs as in the philosophical and religious institutions of man; the power of productivity, position, and authority as in the various areas of business endeavor; and the power of relationship as in the social network of his culture.

However, these higher powers in which man believes and places his faith, fall far short of the highest power that is the true nature of the Divine.

For God is spirit, love, and truth and desires only to be worshipped as such.

Through self-observation, then, man may come to recognize the many gods that he worships: The god of family, the god of duty and obligation, the god of self-sacrifice and denial, the god of rules and regulations, the god of knowledge without wisdom.

Within all of these there is contained a portion of the one truth, but none contain its full measure. For it is not the whole truth, nor is it the whole lie which deceives, but rather the half-truth that fools the very soul of mankind.

In this time of transition, whatever barriers, boundaries, or limitations you've created between yourself and the

Living God, will be removed. Whether it is position, power, relationships, or beliefs, all will be broken and penetrated and crumbled for one intent and for one purpose...

So that you may clearly choose whom it is that you will worship and what it is that you will serve. The one, true, and living God or the many gods of man.

## AWAKENING TO OUR PERSONAL IMAGE OF GOD

Each man formulates a system of beliefs and reacts towards himself and others in accordance with his personal Image of God. To come to know the God he worships, man must learn to observe himself and to reflect on those observations.

What is your Image of God?

Is your god a god of law and justice that metes out punishment for sinners and rewards those who exist in apparent righteousness? Is your god a god of knowledge that pursues understanding itself for its own sake? Is your god a god of truth that is unbending and merciless or one that leads you ever closer to Divine wisdom? Is your god a god of blind faith and obedience that places demands upon you without your understanding? Is your god a god of power and fear that seeks ever to control and manipulate others or is your god a god of love, growth, and mercy?

By examining the way you act towards others you may come to understand your Image of God. For your image of God and your way of dealing with self and others, are indeed one.

If you think one thing and do and say another, then your god is a hypocrite. He is capricious and unpredictible in the way he manifests in the world. If you believe that you can keep secrets hidden from those around you, you believe in a god that is not present and is ignorant of your day-to-day existence. If you believe that there are accidents then you subscribe to a god that is uncaring and random. If you believe that there are things that are impossible, then you believe in a god that is impotent.

By examining your beliefs about yourself and how you act towards others, you may come to know the nature of your personal Image of God.

Once determined, you then have the right to allow this image of God to change as you change in your journey through life. You have the ability to formulate and reformulate this Image and act in accordance with it.

For the God that you worshipped as a child may be different from the God you worship now. Either you have become freer and more expansive or more bound and limited, dependent on the personal experiences that you've attributed to the Divine.

Your personal Image of God then becomes the means through which the Divine may commune, inspire, and guide you in your earthly life. It is the gateway that allows you access through your attunement with this Image into the Divine reality. It is the mechanism through which you have defined what you will and will not allow from your soul into your conscious awareness. It is the means by which you may penetrate the veil of forgetfulness that shrouds your earthly awareness and opens the connections within your own body to your spiritual source.

And it is the means of escape from the wheel-of-life.

Your image of God will provide you with the opportunity to **respond** to your earthly situations in accord with your new-found image of growth, or continue to **react** in repetitive habits, patterns, and beliefs.

## THE THREE FACES OF GOD

So man, then, adheres to one or a portion of all three of these faces or images of God; a god of multiple form or ignorance; a god of mind or duality; and a god of spirit or unity.

In man's earthly expression, the body-mind manifests as ego or personality. It is the actor that plays a role in his earthly drama. The personality experiences pain and pleasure, anguish and happiness, turmoil and silence and is often riddled with a multiplicity of forms and fragmented expressions.

There is the man who plays the role of worker and provider. There is the man who is the husband. There is the man who is the father. The man who is the son to his earthly parents and the brother to his siblings. There is the man who is the friend, the counsellor, the advisor, the repairman, the cook, and so on and on and on.

In each of man's variety of expressions, in each of the different environments, situations, or circumstances, his persona often changes to accomodate. He often reacts to each situation in accordance with his old habits and patterns and is bound by the memories of this or previous lives that continually compels him to repeat and reinforce them.

In this way, this man is in a state of darkness, illusion, ignorance, or forgetfulness about his true nature and the god that this man worships is the god of multiple forms and expressions.

The heart (or unconscious mind) is the messenger of man's earthly drama and, as such, relays experiences from the soul to the conscious or body-mind and from the body-mind back to the soul, most often when the mind of the body is asleep.

In this way, the heart-mind is caught in duality for it partakes of both the Divine and the earthly realities. It takes instructions from both the soul and the body-mind of man, and in this sense, serves two masters. The heart-mind will either hate the one and love the other, or love the one and hate the other.

Thus, it is within the heart that the intensity of the battle between the soul and the personality of man is taking place, for this center is where the heavenly light of the soul is struggling with the darkness of man's earthly kingdoms.

The soul of man is the producer, director, and dispassionate observor of the earthly drama.

As the producer of the earthly drama, the soul is that aspect of the individual that carries the spark of life and allows that life to manifest. At the same time, a portion of the soul continually resides in the spiritual realms and bears witness to the Divine reality. It knows the purpose, mission, and learning required for its earthly incarnation and it strives ever to guide and awaken the body-mind of man.

As the director in earthly life, the soul orchestrates situations that the body-mind needs to experience for the growth and learning of the soul.

The soul of man is in constant communication with other souls, both incarnate and discarnate. Through these communications, it orchestrates learning situations with those others by directing them to the body-mind of this soul through unconscious urges, intuitions, and instructions that it plants within the heart.

The soul then, in essence, sets the stage and attracts the appropriate players who would provide an opportunity for the soul, by way of its body-mind, to experience a learning or lesson.

If the opportunity is not handled by the body-mind in accordance with the soul's purpose or ideal, then the situation or circumstance is repeated. It may appear to conscious awareness as different circumstances and different players in the drama, but the lesson needed by the body-mind and the soul remains the same.

As a dispassionate observer, the soul acts as a guardian angel. And in this sense, due to the gift of free will, the soul of man cannot impose. It can only work in consort with other souls and beings in the etheric and in the earth, to continually provide an opportunity for the body-mind to escape from its earthly bondage and break its self-limiting reactions from the past.

The soul continually calls to the body-mind or personality to see a new and better way to express. But if the body-mind possesses so little attunement that it cannot hear the messages in its dreams, prayers, and meditations, then there is little recourse but to impact the body-mind through earthly trauma and crisis.

In this time of transition, the soul of man is descending and striving to merge with the body-mind of man. The battle raging in man's heart is between the thoughts, beliefs, and determination of the soul in conflict with the thoughts, beliefs, and desires of his body.

For those who continue to seek the light, the result will be a cleansing and a witnessing to the thoughts and desires of their spiritual reality and, through this process, the body-mind or personality of the individual, will be totally transformed.

Thus, through conscious attunement of the body-mind and heart-mind to the soul, through self-observation, self-study, and introspection, through formulating a personal Image of God and then allowing your principles, beliefs, and actions to flow from this image, you can move your attention towards the Divine reality and oneness and remove it from the realms of manifestation and earthly thought alone.

Your image of God is the way in which you can prepare yourself in this time of transition. It is the ideal to which you can aspire, whether Jesus, Buddha, Krishna, Lao-Tze, or others. It must be real and pragmatic in your life and ever change as your personal experiences and your beliefs change.

If your Image of God does not allow you to experience more growth, joy, peace, love, and a sense of wonder, then it is a sign that your image must be re-interpreted and re-examined.

For God is light. God is energy. God is love. God is creative expression in the earth. Each are as soul-specks and carry within them the spark and life of the Divine. And as such, all were made, from the very beginning, in the likeness and the Image of God.

As you grow in understanding towards the mind of the Divine, the image of God you hold is that which you can become in the earth.

## 2.4  OBSTACLES TO SOUL GROWTH

Over the past 30 years, the children and all those who sought the light, have been prepared for this final decade of the millennium.

Each has been given the "tools" - physically, emotionally, and mentally - through their personal search for truth. Each has evolved into a greater understanding through personal development or through gifts that were given to them from the spirit. Each has been placed in the right set of circumstances, relationships, and place for this time.

Each has been given opportunities to learn the lessons that his soul required and a unique set of obstacles to negotiate and overcome that would allow his soul-self to more fully express in the earth. And each of these obstacles could be viewed as either problems or opportunities, stumbling blocks or stepping stones, barriers or doorways, that will lead him to ever greater understanding and growth.

These personal obstacles could be physical wherein the body suffers from illness, disease, excessive pollutants, or some form of disability. They could be emotional obstacles wherein there is an ignorant callousness, una-wareness, or non-acceptance of feelings and desires. They could be mental challenges wherein there is confu-sion, lack of ability to concentrate or focus, and a lack of introspection and self-observation. Or they could be spiritual obstacles wherein there is a lack of purpose, hope, love, or peace.

But the chief obstacle that prevents the growth and unfoldment of the soul of man into fuller relationship with his body-mind is FEAR.

Fear is the greatest destructive force to man's spiritual and mental development. Fear destroys the very organism of man by impeding the circulation of blood, nerve messages to the various systems, and cellular activity. All functioning of assimilation, resuscitation, and elimination are distorted in the presence of fear.

Fear takes the light of the vitality and life force of the body and paralyzes its natural circulation in the body of man. The root cause of much that retards man's spiritual growth is fear, for it is the father of anger, vengeance, pride, bitterness, resentments, doubts, worries, condemnation, denial, and deception towards self and others.

In this time of transition when the soul-will and the bodily desires are out of alignment, fear with all its children will result in man's conscious awareness.

There are many kinds of fear within the earthly experience of man. There is his fear of natural and unnatural things. There is his fear of gaining and losing himself and others. There is his fear of circumstances, situations, and transitions and his fear of fear itself. All these different aspects of fear within man can be blended and merged into two "faces" of fear that serve to retard and paralyze his spiritual growth and unfoldment. These two "faces" of fear are:

Man's fear of death and man's fear of life.

## MANKIND'S FEAR OF DEATH

When man first walked on the face of the earth over a million years ago, the law of self-preservation was written into his earthly expression and became an instinctive drive in his conscious and unconscious awareness.

This law or desire for earthly self-preservation is, in this day, an obstacle to the involution of man's soul-self and, therefore, needs to be overcome and transcended. This desire for self-preservation causes the body-mind to fear anything or any situation that could lead to its death. Whether the death is to the body or to its own self-image or personality, the threat of death will cause a reaction of fear.

The adrenals (third center), which is the custodian of this law of self-preservation, responds and the entire body is readied to react to a perceived threat through fleeing or fighting.

When the "source" or location of the threat cannot easily be identified (as in this time of transition), the body-mind or personality still continues to react in fear. The same influences that were previously constructive and desirable, now become destructive to his physical and mental bodies.

For the "source" of all of man's fears cannot be found outside of man, but rather can be found within him.

Death is change and transition and, in these times of changes, the fear of death in man leads him to maintain and retain the things of the past rather than to allow, search for, and partake of that which is fresh and new and contains an inherent risk to his self-image or personality.

There is an inner awareness in the children of the light that the path of spiritual growth that they walk will lead them to a risk of death on one or more levels of their being. There is a feeling about them and within them that they will die. They know that something must die in order for new life to permeate their beings, but there still remains a sense of reluctance and a resistance to releasing the past.

The methods, then, by which man maintains sameness or habitual reactions in his earthly life are through avoidance, suppression, compromise, and abdication.

Man will instinctively avoid any situation that poses a threat to him physically or to his self-image or personality.

If, by chance, he finds himself in a situation that is threatening to his self-image and the relationships upon which this self-image depends, he will attempt to suppress and deny his intuitive and emotional reactions and strive to maintain the status-quo as best he can.

But when the pain of continual suppression exceeds the pain contained in the fear of death of his self-image and its dependent relationships, then he will witness to what he truly thinks, feels, and perceives about the situation.

Once he shares his truth, however, fear and guilt may once again overcome him and there may be a movement, both within and without, towards compromise for self and others.

Many children of the light are in a state of confusing, dismaying, and often unfulfilling compromise. This compromising state of awareness, for all intents and purposes, causes them to bear witness to the half-truths that compromise alone can bring.

These methods of avoidance, suppression, and compromise are all set in the context of abdicating responsibility for self on all levels of man's being. Of greatest concern to those in the etheric realms is man's abdication of responsibility for his spiritual growth and seeking of the truth.

## OVERCOMING OUR FEAR OF DEATH

To co-operate with the intent of the etheric or Divine rather than resist the closer approach of the soul to the body-mind, you must first turn around, convert, and face yourself and all of your fears. You must seek to confront all of your pains and all of your illusions concerning the death of your earthly self and all that this may entail.

Avoidance, suppression, and compromise will no longer be effective nor viable in this time of transition.

You must begin to awaken to all of your thoughts, feelings, and perceptions that comprise your truth and have the courage to bear witness to it. If the witnessing to your truth leads to pain for yourself and for others around you, then know that there is a pain that leads to life and growth and a pain that leads to death and contraction.

The confusion that so often resides within your hearts is that both of these pains may feel and appear to be the same.

For know that God is truth. If you bear witness with a loving intent to the portion of the truth that has been entrusted into your care, the pain that you and those others will experience is the pain that will lead to growth.

This law is universal: like begets like. If in bearing witness to your truth you act out of fear, the children of this action and the fruits of your labours will be more fear, doubt, worry, anger, confusion, and guilt.

But if in bearing witness to your truth you act out of love, then the fruits of your labours will be, must be, more love, peace, hope, grace, kindness, gentleness.

These fruits of the spirit will manifest first within your own heart and then in those others with whom you interact. This will happen, not in the moment, but in the course of time. For one must learn to be patient and wait upon the Lord and His laws to manifest.

A seed planted in the earth will take from weeks to months to move from germination, rooting in the darkness of the earth, prior to emerging into the light of day. In this same way, the seed-thought of a loving intent planted in another's heart (unconscious mind) will take time before it emerges into the light of their conscious awareness.

Those others may struggle in their own darkness and dance with their own shadows of pain, agony, and fear. But if the action was through a loving-intent, then you must develop a faith that this action will yield more love in the lives of those others in time.

For the law of the Lord of the universes is perfect.

You must then accept personal responsibility for the situation in which you find yourself and for all the consequences that may flow from your decisions.

For the Divine never imposes, but seeks always to provide man an opportunity, an option, a means of escape from earthly bondage. The gift of free or personal will was given to all those who inhabit the earth. Man must choose in this time of change for no one will be able, nor will they be allowed, to choose for him.

But there is help. There is assistance. There is guidance and validation. There will be an answer for all of your prayers if you simply remember to call to the Divine.

## MANKIND"S FEAR OF LIFE

There is, within the heart of man, a fear that acts as a barrier or an obstacle to his growth that is the fear of growth itself.

For God is life. God is growth. God is the fulfillment of all desires.

However, to allow the spirit of life that is contained within your own soul to enter your conscious awareness, there must be change.

For no one may enter the kingdom of heaven with his feet firmly planted on earthly clay and the kingdom of heaven cannot enter anyone until all their obstacles that prevent its descent are removed. One of the major obstacles within the body and mind of man is his fear of God, life, and change.

If you desire that the spirit of God bear witness to your life, then He will descend and walk with you. If you step towards the spirit of the Divine, the spirit of the Divine will step towards you. And in this process, your life will be transformed.

But man fears his own transformation and believes himself to be unworthy of allowing God into his own presence.

God is life and life is change and all contain within them, in the very essence and core of their beings, a spark of the Divine. In this way all are His children. All are worthy of their Divine heritage. Each must simply awaken, attune, and allow Him to have His way with you.

All of your obstacles and fears may be more easily overcome if you link the facing and overcoming of your fear with a higher purpose or Divine intent. By striving to attune and become your Image of God in the earth, all your fears will, in time, be removed from your awareness.

The children of the light will have an innate desire to blend their image of self and their Image of God and make them one in purpose, belief, and action. They desire to become the best that they can be for God, themselves, and others; to keep on keeping on, trying always, even in the face of obstacles and adversity, to become their Image of God.

By giving your attention, energy, and love to your image you must, in time, become it. This Image of God will descend and blend and you will put-on this image and bring it into your daily life as an actor assumes a new role.

This emerging self, as opposed to your previous veneers and fragmentations, will be intertwined with your soul which is, without a doubt, your true Image of God.

In this way, all of your fears and obstacles will be overcome.

## AN AID TO OVERCOMING YOUR OBSTACLES

Those in the heavens have come to aid in this impending conversion, transformation, and healing of the planetary consciousness. A spin has begun in the ethers that is seeking to aid in the removal of the physical and mental pollution from man's nature and will allow the way to be prepared within him for his spiritual emergence.

This spin will allow the children who have sought the light, to face themselves in every way and give them an opportunity to heal on every level of their being.

This etheric spin is light and energy from the Divine and, carries within it, a healing process that has not been seen on the face of the earth for thousands of years. In this time of transition, this healing gift of the spirit is flowing into the earth to aid the body, mind, and soul of mankind.

## 2.5 PERSONAL WHOLISTIC HEALING "THE ETHERIC SPIN"

The path of evolution of man's conscious awareness ever ascending into greater relationship with his Creator, is like a spiral wending its way ever upward into the mind of the Divine.

The path of involution of man's Divine awareness is also like a spiral that strives to descend to meet man's conscious awareness at whatever level of purpose and understanding is required for communion.

The etheric spin or heavenly revolution is a Divine vibration and energy that is spiraling downwards, since August of 1987, onto the earthly framework.

As this spin descends, it is perceived as a whirlwind of changing thoughts, images, and beliefs. As it continues it's descent, it is felt as a whirlpool of emotions, feelings, and desires. As this spin descends further into the earth, it is experienced as a quickening of the space-time continuum where impacting earthly events  move rapidly through man's conscious awareness and time itself is felt to be compressed.

The purpose of this spin is to aid man in his evolutionary movement upwards towards Divine awareness and will move him from a third to a fourth dimensional expression. The spin will serve to help in removing the earthly pollutants from the hearts and minds of men and prepare him for the sensitization and quickening that will follow in this time of consciousness raising.

For those who choose to maintain their earthly existence and cling to their old habits, beliefs, and patterns of behaviour, they will experience this etheric spin as a merry-go-round or a wheel-of-life that they spin upon.

The spin will move them in circles, ever faster as the decade progresses, causing them to become confused and disoriented about their earthly existence. Situations and events that previously took years to unfold and manifest will now be impacting them daily. Time will seem and is being compressed so much so that 10 to 20 years of previous earthly experience (as in the beginning of this 50 year cycle of transition) is compressed into a single year.

There will be a yearning, by those who have chosen the mundane, for stability. But they will not find it in the systems and structures, nor even in the very planet itself. For there will be continual change all around them.

Unless they choose, at some point in this revolutionary process, to find stability within, they will be overcome by the effects of this continual change from without.

For those who have chosen life and growth, they will experience the etheric spin as a series of rapidly moving wheels and spirals.

## THE PATH OF HEALING

This path of healing will originate in your heart in response to the desires for the Divine that you've held there.

When the spin begins, it will move your body-mind or conscious awareness, first upwards to partake of the heavenly food, strength, and sustenance you may obtain there and then downwards into the depths of your earthly nature.

In your earthly nature, you will face all that you believed yourself to be in this and past incarnations. All your present and past memories that may impede or hinder the life force from circulating freely within you will bubble and froth into your conscious awareness.

This circular and spiraling movement of etheric energy, once begun, will continue unerringly towards its completion and your body-mind will be moved rapidly through a number of stages or states of awareness.

First, there is an event or situation or circumstance that acts as the seed of the spin. The event can be sourced from any of the seven levels of your being and the event is impacting.

This event will cause you to move from a state of ignorance or forgetfulness to a state of recognition of an issue or a condition you need to face that is embodied and is the seed-meaning of the event. It becomes the means of awakening you to an issue or area in your life that you could not previously perceive.

Once you recognize your condition or issue, you move into a state of reflection wherein you begin to examine all the factors that lead up to this issue or condition. You will reflect on all your past patterns that may have been dissimilar in form, but similar in meaning to the condition or issue you are currently experiencing.

The intensity of the thoughts and feelings within this spin will be due to the gathering of all of your past life patterns in the wake of this spin that, in a sense, resonate with your current event in meaning. The nature of these past life patterns may or may not become known to your conscious awareness. But be assured, they are never-the-

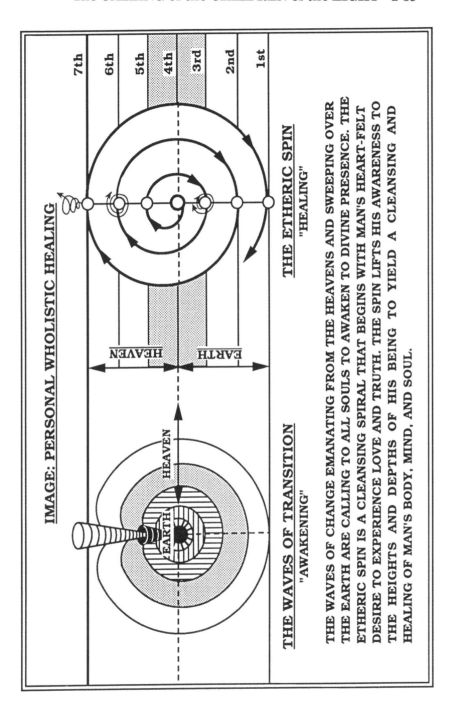

IMAGE: PERSONAL WHOLISTIC HEALING

THE ETHERIC SPIN
"HEALING"

THE WAVES OF TRANSITION
"AWAKENING"

THE WAVES OF CHANGE EMANATING FROM THE HEAVENS AND SWEEPING OVER THE EARTH ARE CALLING TO ALL SOULS TO AWAKEN TO DIVINE PRESENCE. THE ETHERIC SPIN IS A CLEANSING SPIRAL THAT BEGINS WITH MAN'S HEART-FELT DESIRE TO EXPERIENCE LOVE AND TRUTH. THE SPIN LIFTS HIS AWARENESS TO THE HEIGHTS AND DEPTHS OF HIS BEING TO YIELD A CLEANSING AND HEALING OF MAN'S BODY, MIND, AND SOUL.

7th  6th  5th  4th  3rd  2nd  1st

HEAVEN  EARTH

HEAVEN

EARTH

less present with you in the total experiencing of this event.

From reflection you will be given an opportunity to transform your beliefs about the event and all the past events that are associated with them. Will you react to this new event as in your past, or will you respond to it in accordance with your image of God?

In your perceptions, the events and experiences of your past are unchangeable. That is, the space, time, thoughts, and feelings will remain and are recorded in memory for all time. But each perception contains an experience and the beliefs you held about that experience. The key, then, to transformation is this:

**THE "EVENT" OR EXPERIENCE CANNOT BE CHANGED. WHAT CAN AND MUST BE ALLOWED TO CHANGE, HOWEVER, IS YOUR BELIEF ABOUT THAT EXPERIENCE.**

This is the stage where the struggle and battle occurs. Old patterns versus new patterns;  body-mind versus soul-mind; old system versus the new system; image of self versus your image of God. Which will it be?

Once decided, then you will move from transformation to a state of application wherein you will be given an opportunity - on whatever level required - to confirm and validate your decision.

If you've chosen to react in old and often inoperative ways to this event, then the spin will feel like a wheel that turns and, in this movement, grants you another event or opportunity to alter your old ways.

If you remain consistent in your choices and desires for life and growth, events will repeat over and over again until you apprehend the meaning and the lesson of it, even though the form of the event may change.

If you've chosen to respond to this event in new ways that are in accord with your image of God, then the spin will be initially like a wheel that revolves and brings with this revolution, another opportunity to test and apply this new way in your life.

Once successfully applied in the earth, once the test is completed, once the lesson is learned, the spin will feel like a spiral that moves you ever closer into relationship with the Divine.

This cycle of ignorance, recognition,reflection, transformation, and application is repeated over and over again until a cleansing of memories - and the beliefs associated with them - are dealt with and removed from your body and heart minds.

In striving to transform your beliefs you will in time align with the mind of the Divine, but only if you consistently choose and desire God, life, and growth.

For remember, knowledge, when coupled with an experience of that knowledge, gives man his beliefs. Man's beliefs, when coupled with an experience of those beliefs, gives man his faith.

This etheric spin is aiding the children who are seeking the light in obtaining and retaining faith in the Divine.

For where is it that the Divine has promised to meet you? Is it in the marketplace? Is it in the buildings and structures and systems of man? Or is it within your body and your mind that could be as a temple of the living God?

The stability that the sons of earth, who have chosen the mundane yearn for, will be found to reside within the very hearts of the children of the light.

As the storms of emotions and the winds of change billow and froth around mankind, these children will be as the eye of the storms and will serve as the very foundation stones of peace upon which the new order, the new harmony, the very kingdom of heaven may descend and reside on the earth.

## INSIGHTS AND SUGGESTIONS ON THE HEALING-CLEANSING PROCESS

No amount of preparation can fully prepare you for the intensity of the emotions and the anxiety that accompany the process of dying to your own self-image or personality.

To prepare the way for the emergence of the soul, the veneers, images, and fronts of your various fragmented forms of earthly expression need to be broken into pieces - some discarded, some added, and then all rearranged - into a new form.

And this new form will allow the individuality of your soul to more fully express through your personality in the earth.

The healing and cleansing process is then the dying to all these fragmented expressions, followed by reflection, then followed by integration and synthesis or rebirth. In this sense, this process will allow you to be reborn into new life in the earth.

However, to aid in this process of dying to self, the spirit of truth within will continually direct and bear witness to a series of surprises or events that are designed to shock and dislodge your old habits and past patterns of reaction.

For it is true that the same "tools" of body and mind that helped you in one phase of your spiritual growth and development, are the same tools that become the hindrances, barriers, and obstacles in the next.

Often, man is entangled in binding habits, rituals, and forms that become his masters and not his servants. The call is then to search for the meaning and the spirit that stands behind these behaviours and to bear witness to them. To continually look for the light, life, and love of the Divine in all the thought and actions of men.

For the spirit of love is not one of clinging and holding, but is one of giving, releasing, and acceptance. Like the sun that gives of its light, life, and warmth to all those of the earth without exception, the spirit of love gives to all those who seek and are willing to accept it.

Ask, affirm, and invoke the presence of the Divine in your process and indeed, His spirit will bear witness with your own. Attune through inner prayer and meditation. In this light, allow whatever is occurring to occur and respond to it in accord with your image of God. Expect the best from this spirit of love and strive to continually accept with grace all that flows into your conscious awareness.

In this way, the burdens that you experience, can be lightened by those who seek to aid in the heavens.

## OBSERVATIONS ON THE PATH OF HEALING

The etheric spin is but one form of healing that is on the earthly-framework at this time. It is a guided and compressed version, because of the times, but it is only one method of the one force that continually strives to heal and make all whole again.

For whether the healing is physical through man's use and application of his knowledge of technology and science as in the medical institutions, or whether it is of the psychiatric, psychological, or sociological treatments or therapy to aid in healing the mind of man, or whether it is of counselling or support in the form of groups to aid in the healing of man's emotional body, or whether it is faith healing, psychic healing, or spiritual healing for the soul of man...

Regardless of the shape or the form:

## ALL HEALING COMES FROM THE ONE SOURCE.

All healing is of the Divine, whether mankind is consciously aware of it or not. All that man can do is to establish the conditions in body, mind, and soul that will allow this healing and this journey into wholeness.

The etheric spin is a unique form of healing for this time, but only if man allows it to occur, to him and through him.

All levels of man are impacted by this etheric process. Every center is touched, awakened, and cleansed. Every center is in balance and in harmony so long as the desire for God, life, love, and growth in man is maintained.

The three principle avenues of escape from man's three

dimensional confinement is through his solar plexus, spiritual eye, or crown chakra. Each time he sleeps, man leaves his body to follow the path of this universal space-time spiral that is the royal road that connects all dimensions.

And where man's awareness finally comes to rest amongst all those dimensions is solely dependent on the purposes, desires, and motivations that he holds in his heart.

This spiral path is universal, but it is also personal and only if the etheric spiral begins in the heart of man can this balanced process cleanse the whole seven dimensions of which man is comprised. Beginning anywhere else, there is imbalance and the eventual merging of his spiritual and earthly nature cannot occur.

All desires, in this process, then merge into one desire, and that is to know and be one with the Divine. All purposes then merge into one purpose, and that is to serve the living God. All beliefs then flow from this merging of purpose and desire. And all actions will flow into earthly expression from these beliefs.

Then you will be healed. Then you will be made whole again in your own eyes and in the eyes of the Divine.

And this is the meaning behind the calling of the children of the light, for it is a calling to be made whole again in Him who is the maker and Creator of all things.

## A QUESTION OF LOVE

As with one voice they all had cried,

"O Lord, When will we with certainty know
the power and beauty of our own soul?"

And to them all the Lord replied;

**When the Seeds of Truth that I have sown,
Blossom and bear Fruit inside your Bones.**

**When all that is Outside is found Within,
When your Body and Mind are Purged of Sin.**

**When you have Given as you have Received,
When your Gaining exceeds the Losses Grieved.**

**When all that is Earthy has become Divine,
For You - and for All - This is the Final Sign.**

**Then, my Children, you will surely Know,
The Shape and Texture of your own Soul.**

**I in You and You in Me,
Together, you and I will be,**

**Truthful, Joyous, Peaceful and Whole.
When, My Child, You know your Soul.**

## 2.6 SPIRITUAL EMERGENCE

The path to enlightenment that the children of the light and the sons of man - who ever seek the light of the Divine - walk in this time of transition is the same path that has been followed for tens of thousands of years by all the great mystics, prophets, and visionaries.

The only difference in this time is that, what once took a lifetime to learn, has now been accelerated so that these lessons can be learned in days, weeks, or months.

The path to enlightenment begins by preparing the way within you for the entrance of the Divine. Preparation, in its essence, is to do whatever is required by you, in your body and heart minds, to allow them to be fit for you to meet and entertain your image of God.

In response to the earnestness of your desire and preparation, you are given an experience of the heavenly reality that serves to awaken you to a new way of seeing and believing. This awakening is usually some supernatural event, such as a vision, dream, healing, manifestation, or illumination that seems to furnish a way of freeing yourself from earthly bondage. The experience is usually momentary, but is sufficient in length to stimulate the desire to make this momentary experience of the Divine more permanent.

On the strength of the spiritual food and the personal experiences of the Divine, there follows a purging and a cleansing of all obstacles that prevents closer relationship with the Divine and all that impedes the circulation of light and love.

This cleansing process has been called purgation, healing, the forgiveness of sins, redemption, and the dark night of the soul. All debts and obligations are felt to have been paid at the conclusion of this phase of enlightenment.

Finally, your soul-self descends and, in a sense, repossesses your body and heart minds in a type of union or marriage of your spiritual and earthly natures.

This final descent of the soul into all parts of your body is felt by your conscious awareness as **Spiritual Emergence.**

## FROM KARMA TO GRACE

The earthly-framework was established and is maintained by Divine or universal laws. These laws that govern man's expressions are reflections of the one and immutable law of love.

As this one and Divine law descends into the realms of manifestation, eventually arriving on the third dimensional earthly expression, it appears as three distinct sets or groupings: physical or natural laws; mental laws; and spiritual laws.

These Divine or universal laws are constant and unchanging for they are one facet of the very nature of the Divine. They continue to operate regardless of man's beliefs or ignorance of their existence.

Due to the soul's manifestation in the earth, there arises a sense of hierarchy to these laws. The physical laws can be overcome by man's use of the mental laws. And the mental laws can be overcome by his use of the spiritual laws.

If man allows himself to be governed by the physical or natural laws alone, then the law of gravity continues to pull him to the earth. But the law of gravity can be overcome in the experience of man with his understanding and application of the mental laws.

The corresponding law of the mind to the earthly law of gravity is the law of attraction. Through his choices and beliefs acting with and through this law of attraction, man may come to understand that levity is preferred to the gravity of the earthly-framework and, thereby, overcome the physical limitations of that earthly law.

For thought overcomes all space-time limitations, and Spirit overcomes all the limitations of thought.

The Divine or universal laws establish the framework or the rules of the game of the earthly drama. Man's personal will or determination works with and through these laws to create his earthly reality, experiences, and memories.

When a free will decision is made the action and operation and fulfillment of that decision - acting through Divine law - is termed (in man's understanding) destiny.

In the beginning, the First Cause desired that the light, which resided in the all-knowing and aware darkness, expand and begin the song of creation. The cause then, was in the desire that was patterned through Divine mind into the manifestation of creation.

The reflection of this original movement in the heavenly realms is known on the earth as the law of karma or cause and effect.

The memory of man's manifested experiences and outcomes of his choices acting through universal principles or law is karma. The meeting and re-experiencing of the meaning, lessons, or memories required by the soul is also called karma.

For each must meet himself and either pay or reap the rewards of his past determinations.

The current state of ignorance, error, sin, or illusion that man finds himself and the earth in, is not due to an imposition of the Divine, but rather springs from man's own choices in his present or past incarnations. This is also true of his state of purity, love, and illumination.

The evolutionary movement of man's understanding in the distant past was to seek, know, co-operate with and fulfill the law of karma or cause and effect. This law is like the wheel-of-life that endlessly spins and creates circumstances and situations for man to learn the lessons needed for his soul.

The opportunity provided in this time of transition is that man may meet himself on all levels of his being and pay all his debts and obligations owed under this law of cause and effect. However, the method of how this debt needed to be repaid has changed over the past two thousand or so years.

Since the son of God (that one known as Jesus the Christ) walked, ministered, and was a living example or pattern of how this law of karma should be overcome...

## ALL MAN'S BURDENS HAVE THE POTENTIAL TO BE LIGHTENED.

In living the law he became it. In his death and resurrection he showed that he overcame the law of karma and established in man's conscious and unconscious awareness for all time, the law of harmony or grace.

The weight of man's self-created karmic burdens can be lifted with the establishment of this new access or way to oneness with the Divine.

For no one may go to the Divine Father except through the Christ consciousness or mind of the Divine.

The children of the light through preparation, awakening, and cleansing are fulfilling the law of karma. In spiritual emergence it is their movement from karma to the way of grace.

Within the body of these children, the awakening is that of the pineal, crown chakra, or Christ consciousness center into their conscious awareness. The secretions from the awakening of this gland enter the blood and transform the very cells and tissues of all parts of man's body. The regeneration of the body is normally an earthly cycle of seven years. But with the awakening of the Divine consciousness center, this spiritual regeneration could take from minutes, hours, to days to be accomplished for it transcends physical limitations of the body cycle of man.

The awareness of oneness with the Divine then begins to descend to and through the spiritual eye of man and then downward through the heart and body of man.

As it descends, it leaves in its wake, the fruits of peace, hope, harmony, and love.

## THE AFFECTS OF SPIRITUAL EMERGENCE

The impact of your spiritual or soul emergence will be felt on all levels of your being.

Spiritually, you will begin to sense and feel the tangible presence of the Divine. You may experience a growing connectedness and purposefulness to your life. You may begin to hear voices in your heart and mind. You may experience visions, dreams, and visitations of guides, divine beings, or other angelic forms. You may apprehend inspirations, illuminations, and divine ideas into your conscious remembrance.

At times, you may feel very lonely and alone, for there may be few with whom you can share your innermost feelings and experiences, few that could and would accept without judgement.

Mentally and emotionally, you may feel vulnerable and confused. Your ability to focus and concentrate on your duties and obligations may be severely impaired. At times, you may feel that you are suffering from some form of mental or emotional illness or derangement. That all your Divine experiences are the product of an overactive imagination and you may struggle to suppress or deny them.

Others may counsel you to seek mental-emotional therapy or drugs to aid you through your time of turmoil and tribulation. Still others may suggest that this is of the darkness and not a response from the heavens to your desire for the light.

For in your heart of hearts you are aware that this is a calling of the Divine, but you may struggle with feelings of deep unworthiness and low self-esteem.

You may feel that you are dying and experience all the thoughts and feelings that accompany that process in the earth. There may be an experience of a terrifying darkness that aggravates your feelings of hopelessness, loneliness, and despair that occurs even in the midst of your search for the light.

As this process of emergence progresses, your perspectives will begin to change. What was once the center of importance in your life will be the center no longer.

Physically, you may experience heart throbs or pain and a general feeling of anxiety and may suffer from attacks of that same. Your vision may be affected. You may not be able to focus properly and may experience double vision that will lead you to believe that you need an aid or correction.

You may feel a pressure, pain, or difficulty in the medulla oblongata (where the spinal column meets the skull) and various other portions of your brain that could cause extreme headaches.

The emergence will impact your body's metabolism and you may experience hot and cold flashes through your central and peripheral nervous systems. Your diet may change dramatically with a growing inablity to digest and assimilate certain foods and beverages that you may have enjoyed before. Your eliminations will be affected as the body responds to the transformation on other levels of your being. The body may retain fluids for a period of time and there will be a general swelling that would be most noticeable in the feet and hands.

And there may be a general feeling of mental-emotional-physical exhaustion and fatigue.

As the spirit continues its descent and your soul's awareness emerges into your consciousness, remember that this too shall pass. The duration of the emergent process is dependent on each individual, for each is unique and may warrant a different sequence of events and their respective timing.

In the wake of this descent, there will arise the fruits of the spirit in your heart: faith, peace, hope, charity, illumination, and clarity of thought. There will, then, arise in your conscious awareness the gifts in earthly expressions of the spirit; kindness, gentleness, long-suffering, patience, humility, goodness, equanimity.

As this state of alignment and attunement progresses, remember to remain awakened to the purpose. Remember that those in the heavens await your call, your request, your plea for help...and they will come...and they will aid.

Remember to invoke the presence of the Divine. Remember to focus your thoughts on the majesty and magnificence of that great love, and remember to act lovingly in the earth in harmony and accord with what you feel to be your image of God.

For love is giving and love is serving and so long as the light of love flows from the seven centers of your body, nothing of the darkness or mundane earthly thought may enter you again.

Then you may truly be IN the World but not of IT.

## THE SENSITIZATION OF MANKIND

Because the sensitization of man is in opposition to the forces of darkness that seek to pollute his conscious awareness, there will be a profound change in mankind as a result of his spiritual emergence.

The human form will exist much as it does today, but what

will change is man's ability to be simultaneously sensitive to the spiritual and earthly realities. This sensitization will impact man on all levels of his being for it is a change within the very cells of which he is comprised.

Man's metabolism will be altered. His heart will beat at a faster rate. He will become more sensitive to earthly pollutants and may experience headaches and various irritations and rashes of the skin.

Man will become highly intuitive, extremely telepathic, and, if he desires an object or an experience, will be able to manifest these directly from the ethers.

There will be a blending between all man's earthly senses with Divine awareness. Touch will respond with a tingling sensation. The eyes will become more sensitive to the colours of the ethers as the spiritual eye blends with the carnal eyes. Man will taste, not only with his earthly tongue, but with his spiritual tongue as well. Man will be able to hear the music of the spheres blended with the rhythms of the earth.

For through this time of transition, materialism will no longer be man's foundations, but rather his being will be founded on spirituality.

The greater portion of these gifts, for the majority of mankind, will not occur for two or even three generations. But for the children who seek the light, they are occurring in this very day.

These children of the light, after completing their work on the earth, will move into different consciousnesses and states of awareness. They will move as a group, bonded by a covenant with the Divine to ever strive to illuminate the darkness.

# IMPACTING OUR RELATIONSHIPS

## 3.1 SOUL RELATIONSHIPS are MADE in HEAVEN

In the earthly-framework, man experiences a variety of different relationships. These relationships embrace a diverse spectrum from relations with himself and others to relations within vocations and institutions, circumstances and situations, things, times, places, and dimensions.

Each relationship carries with it a unique characteristic, learning, and understanding from the superficial and sublime to the deeply impacting and intimate, from the casual and brief to the seemingly eternal, and from the shallowness of polite acquaintance to being as one with that other.

Regardless of their shape, texture, or form, all relationships of every nature begin and end in the heavens.

For each soul was born in the heavens. Each soul is loved and beloved. Each soul is monitored, observed, guided, and aided by the messengers, stewards, and helpmates of the Divine - neither to control nor to manipulate - but watched as a loving father or mother looks upon the achievements and life's progress of their children with only the desire and the longing to help them live their lives with more joy and fulfillment.

Regardless of how far souls may stray from the path of truth and love, each will be sought after and pursued by those in the heavens. Each will be given the opportunity, time and time and time again, to return into a fuller awareness of their Divine and spiritual nature.

For the Father-Mother-God has willed that no soul shall be lost. No soul shall ever be abandoned nor shall it ever be forgotten.

So that, in the kingdom of heaven, the least of the souls that walks on the face of planet earth in this day, is as important and as special and as loved as the greatest soul in all of manifested and unmanifested creation.

Each soul is so unique and perfect and so truly individual in its needs and expressions, that the task each is being called and requested to perform for the Divine in this time of transition on the earth, could not be performed as well by any other soul.

In this way, whether the soul was of the sixth or the seventh vibration matters not in the mind of the Divine, for all souls are his children. All souls, at the core of their being, have a remembrance of their relationship with truth and illumination and carry within them the spark of life Divine.

In the beginning, then, in the heavenly realms, there was only relationship with the First Cause and with all manifested soul-specks and vibrational awarenesses.

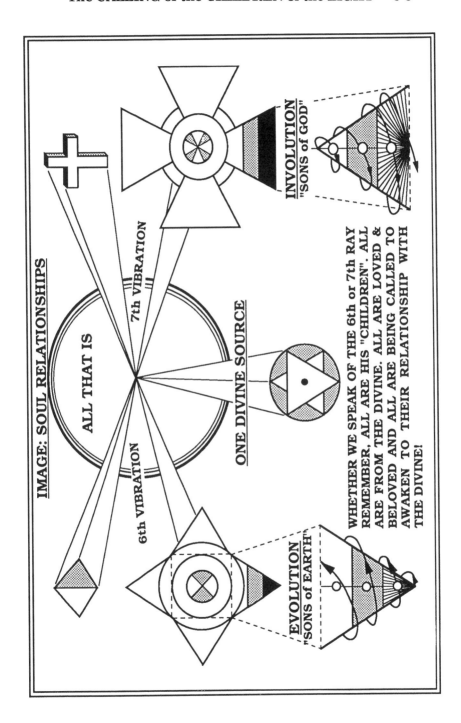

IMAGE: SOUL RELATIONSHIPS

ALL THAT IS

7th VIBRATION

6th VIBRATION

ONE DIVINE SOURCE

INVOLUTION "SONS of GOD"

EVOLUTION "SONS of EARTH"

WHETHER WE SPEAK OF THE 6th or 7th RAY REMEMBER, ALL ARE HIS "CHILDREN". ALL ARE FROM THE DIVINE. ALL ARE LOVED & BELOVED AND ALL ARE BEING CALLED TO AWAKEN TO THEIR RELATIONSHIP WITH THE DIVINE!

Each vibrational awareness knew itself to be as brothers and sisters with one another and in spiritual marriage and union with Divine intent. And each vibration had a special role to play in God's universal song of creation.

The purpose and the path of entrance onto the earthly framework was different for the sixth vibration or the sons of the earth than it was for the seventh vibration or the sons of God.

The purpose, task, or mission for the sons of earth was in essence, to raise the awareness of the five vibrations that comprised the consciousness of the earthly planet over ten million years ago, by blending their higher vibratory Divine awareness with the lower earthly vibrations and elements.

This was an experiment designed to determine if Divine love could merge with, manifest, and overcome three-dimensional physicality. For a variety of reasons, the experiment went askew and man's resulting awareness deviated so far from the original thought and intent in the heavens that the seventh vibration was called on and added to the earthly-framework.

Initially, rather than blending with the earthly elements and evolving with them into higher awareness as was attempted by the sons of earth, the sons of God involved themselves in the earthly-framework. First they appeared as spirit beings or guides and then, much later, as manifestations and incarnations in the earth.

## THE INVOLUTION OF THE SONS OF GOD IN THE EARTH

As the seventh ray approached the sixth vibrational

awareness of the earthly-framework it contained many soul-specks that were bonded with a singular purpose and intent. Their task or mission was to allow the love and light of the Divine, that they carried in the core of their beings, to illuminate the darkness of ignorance and forgetfulness that had dimmed the awareness of man.

Just as the awakening of the fifth chakra can have a tremendous impact on the body, mind, and soul of an individual, the entrance of this seventh vibration had a corresponding impact on the very soul of mankind.

The Lemurian civilization that existed on the earth 100,000 years ago, was most impacted by the addition of this quickened consciousness in the earth. Hope was rekindled. There was high anxiety, not of the negative kind, but of anticipation, wonder, and awe at the manifestations of the Divine. Man was compelled into reflecting on his origins and heritage and began to question the who and what and why of his earthly existence.

As a result, the activity and pace of mankind's earthly development increased dramatically.

However, the fall of the sons of God as they strove to aid mankind in their androgynous states, caused their withdrawal and reformulation of how best to help without the further risk of loss to this seventh vibrational awareness.

There was a lack of knowing in the etheric and angelic realms concerning the best way to accomplish man's awakening. For the differentiation of the souls' vibrations, the veil of forgetfulness that allowed free-will in ignorance rather than the heavenly choice or determination in wisdom and full knowledge, and the limitations and ponderousness of physicality, were all unique experiences to the souls that comprised this seventh vibration.

As a result, some soul-specks were trapped or caught in the earthly drama out of and through their own ignorance.

One soul-speck, of the many contained within this *"branch"* of the seventh vibration, became their spokesman and conferred with the great and Universal Mind on this earthly dilemna. From this meeting of awarenesses, there arose a determination that, in an effort to more closely align with the sons and daughters of the earth, the sons of God would attempt to break or split themselves into two half, but complementary, aspects of their soul.

Since this thought was a new and untested approach it carried with it the risk of further loss to that co-creative seventh vibration that could be used by the Divine to illuminate the darkness. This spokesman soul then volunteered to be the first to incarnate. If the experimental incarnation was successful, then other soul-specks could follow. If unsuccessful and that soul-speck was lost, then the remaining children could devise and formulate yet another plan of rescue.

And so, with the agreement of the Divine, all of the children of the light broke or split themselves from within and placed the light of truth and the flame or spark of life within each "half" of their soul.

All soul-specks split in the spiritual realms about 30,000 years ago, but it was the spokesman soul for the group that initiated the earthly cycle of learning by physically manifesting nearly 25,000 years ago, as the five pairs of primordial "earthly parents" that gave birth to the five races of man.

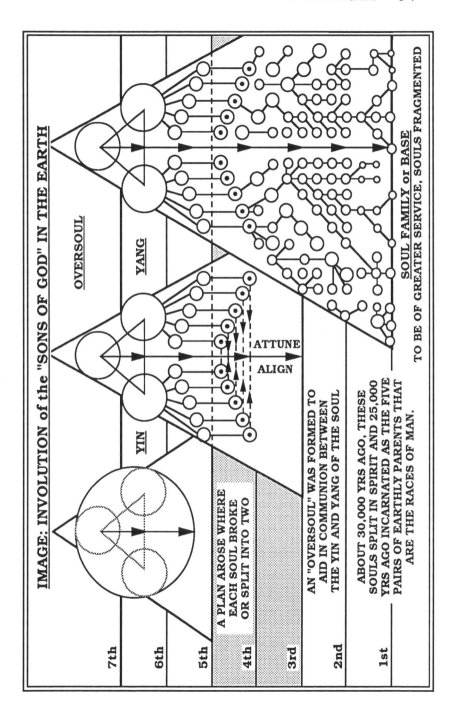

IMAGE: INVOLUTION of the "SONS OF GOD" IN THE EARTH

OVERSOUL

YANG

YIN

ATTUNE

ALIGN

SOUL FAMILY or BASE
TO BE OF GREATER SERVICE, SOULS FRAGMENTED

A PLAN AROSE WHERE EACH SOUL BROKE OR SPLIT INTO TWO

AN "OVERSOUL" WAS FORMED TO AID IN COMMUNION BETWEEN THE YIN AND YANG OF THE SOUL

ABOUT 30,000 YRS AGO, THESE SOULS SPLIT IN SPIRIT AND 25,000 YRS AGO INCARNATED AS THE FIVE PAIRS OF EARTHLY PARENTS THAT ARE THE RACES OF MAN.

7th

6th

5th

4th

3rd

2nd

1st

The original cause or split into yin and yang or receptive and creative aspects of the one soul as it incarnated in the earth, became known (in man's understanding) as twin souls or flames. At the same time that this one soul split into two aspects, there was formed an oversoul or higher self.

The oversoul remained in the heavenly realms of Divine intent and functioned as a communication and a healing link between these two halves of the self-same soul. In this way, the two soul-aspects could reconnect to the Divine through their original light or spirit being knowledge.

Now, the oversoul for the entire spiritual community contained within this seventh vibrational "branch", was the same. It retained the common purpose and Divine intent of that community and, in this same way, the yin and yang aspects of this original cause or spiritual division, was also the same for all of the children of the light.

The image that most often comes to mind for these children when they contemplate the Divine is that of the yin as Divine mother, Divine wisdom, or the "Lady of the Light". The image that comes to mind for the yang component is the Divine teacher, eldest brother, or "The Holy One".

What was common, then, amongst these children was the oversoul and the access to Divine illumination that it contained and the male and female polarities that resulted from their heavenly division. What was unique to each aspect or split-soul was the truth and life of the Divine.

In this way, the split-soul possessed all the attributes that allowed full alignment with the heavens and full alignment with the the sons of the Earth.

Each twin, split, or half-soul retained the desire to be co-creative. It desired to continue to lighten the darkness and to grow and expand its own knowledge and awareness. So great was this desire for expansion and for being of greater and greater service as an instrument of the Divine, that these half-souls split even further.

Every soul, when faced with the space and time and awareness limitations that characterize the earthly-framework, requires patience to come into a fuller awareness of the Divine. But the tremendous desire to be of service to the Divine and mankind, caused these seventh vibrational souls to fragment further from their original or twin soul awareness.

In this way, one portion or fragment of the soul could be manifesting in Egypt at the same time as another portion or fragment experienced Atlantis. Or, when viewed from the etheric, one fragment could be in England in 1500 AD while another soul fragment was in the land now known as Peru in 1500 BC.

For in the spiritual realms there are no space-time limitations and what is important is, not the time, place, or space, but rather the lessons and purpose needed by or accorded to, each soul or soul fragment.

In this manner, more light, love, and truth could be given into the awareness of the soul of mankind by the children of the light.

Each soul fragment, in turn, was also self-sufficient and could, if it so desired, fragment itself even further. This desire was particularly embodied by those souls or soul fragments that were enlightened and desired to be of greater service to mankind. These fragments determined to fragment into the second, third, fourth, and so on generations beyond that of the original or primordial soul-split.

The virtual body of these original soul-specks, through the manifestations of its fragmented aspects, would enlarge and expand with the addition of memories, learnings, and growing awareness. In time and through patience, each soul-speck developed a unique set of abilities, talents, expressions, and vibrations accorded to it by the various members of its soul family or soul base.

Dependent on the determinations of the original soul-speck, each soul family or base could be comprised of a handful of fragments or number in the thousands of unique expressions bonded under a common purpose.

At any moment in earthly space and time, aspects or fragments of the soul could reside and be experiencing the higher spiritual domains while other aspects could be simultaneously incarnating in the deepest depths of earthly expression, while still others could experience the regions, vibrations, or dimensions in-between.

Thus, the SOUL FAMILY of each soul fragment could contain tremendous depth and breadth of experience and abilities.

Each soul fragment is whole in the sense that it has the ability to attune itself to the Divine through alignment with its oversoul. And one soul fragment is not "older" or "newer" than another, for each can trace its Divine lineage to the original vibration of the First Cause by going within and immersing itself in the full knowledge, remembrance, and awareness of that same.

Soul fragments, as well as fragmenting further, could

also seek to join or blend with other souls or soul fragments and combine their unique talents, gifts, and abilities for a particular manifestation or incarnation. Then afterwards, they could part or remain in union, as determined by each soul or soul fragment.

When members of the same soul family come together in various forms of relationship, there is a special bonding and intermixing that occurs through manifestations and incarnations.

In this time of transition, many members of these soul families are incarnate on the earth. What will begin to emerge and awaken within these children is, neither the coming together for common needs, desires, and activities or gathering because of common beliefs...

But what will grow and grow is the desire to gather with and for a common purpose. The result will be a search by many individuals for soul family.

### SPIRITUAL AND KARMIC RELATIONSHIPS

Soul relationships can be of a spiritual intent and nature, a karmic intent or nature, or a blending of these two. All relationships have a commonality in that they are all designed for each individual to meet himself, to learn the lessons of his soul, and to become more aware of his relationship to the Divine.

There are several ways that souls can experience relations. There are relations and inter-relationships within a soul family. There are relationships that form between soul families. And there are karmic or incarnational relationships.

## Relationships within Soul Families

As the soul-speck expands in experience and awareness and fragments more and more, the working relationship between these soul fragments tends to draw some fragmented souls together in a more cohesive way than other fragments.

When this occurs, there evolves a type of covenant or a spiritual promise between soul fragments to aid each other in their growing awareness, illumination, and co-creativity. With this special commitment to one another, these can rightly be called SOUL MATES.

Soul mates can experience one another over and over again in numerous lifetimes or states of awareness to aid each other in their growth. But it will not always be with the same soul mate, for each soul fragment can have many soul mates.

When one experiences a soul-mate relationship, it is often a great relief for there is such understanding and sense of familiarity and easiness of earthly living, that many other aspects of earthly and spiritual dimensions can be examined and developed.

In much the same way, there are brother and sister souls who have such a tremendous understanding of each other, familiarity, and commitment to each other's growth that they feel like, and often have, incarnated as brothers and sisters.

It should be considered a gift to have an experience of a brother or sister soul or soul-mate in any manifestation or incarnation.

The eldest brothers and sisters or the first earthly incarnations of each soul family are called twin souls. The idea of twin souls or twin flames, although conceived within the mind of man, has seldom been experienced in the earthly-framework.

When one part of the light or flame of the original soul meets another, a special state of awareness is given the opportunity to manifest on the earth. A tremendous force is activated that serves to draw them together or to congeal the various other portions of that soul's expression such that all parts begin to link up and align with a higher purpose, to redefine itself, and to potentially manifest in a healing and wondrous ministry in the earth.

Some examples in man's knowledge and history were Osiris and Isis in Egypt. Adam and Eve in Eden with the same soul as Jesus and Mary in Palestine. Quatzlcoatl and his beloved mate in the Mayan lands. Buddha and his beloved disciple in India. And Krishna and his beloved mate in the Aryan lands.

Each combining and rejoining and alignment of these twin souls was a gift to those souls and a gift to the soul of mankind.

Even though twin souls have been an unaccustomed experience on the earthly-framework, more and more of these souls will merge, blend, and align through their original cause through their oversoul and to the Divine.

What is and will be occurring in this time, is that the children of the light are completing their karmic cycle and growing into greater awareness and fulfillment of their covenant with the Divine to aid mankind.

The covenant or promise from the Divine to these children is that they will be merged, re-joined, and re-unified with all of their splits and fragmentations and rise to a higher awareness, never needing again to return to the earthly-framework.

One aspect of this re-union and re-joining of the soul will be a greater and greater rate - as never before seen in the earth - of the merging and the blending of these twin souls into harmony and alignment with the Divine.

## Relationships between Soul Families

On and within the "branch" of the seventh vibration that was added to the earthly-framework, there were many soul-specks and many kinds of vibrations.

Just as there are different cells within the body of man to perform different tasks, so within the seventh vibration there were different needs and therefore, slightly different resonances within that seventh vibration. These different soul-specks were aware in different and unique ways, but all shared a common purpose and intent.

Two soul bases or families, then, can be part of the same purpose or intent, but be of slightly different vibration. When souls from these slightly different vibrations meet, they are said to be of the same soul fabric, or the same spiritual group or community, for their purpose or intent is the same, but they are not of the same soul family.

The joining in relationship with one of the same spiritual group or fabric still retains the sense of familiarity, but it is neither as great nor as inspirational in manifesting (in other ways beyond the relationship) as it would be if one was with a member of one's own soul family.

## Karmic Relationships

Through karmic or incarnational interaction, some souls become bonded to another soul family or to other souls to help clarify, blend, and monitor their development.

What occurs then, are very karmic relationships as opposed to those which have a spiritual or soul intent.

Karma, memory, or learnings can develop between individuals who are not of the same soul family or even of the same soul fabric. The purpose of these interactions is to aid and stimulate the growth and insight with each other. To help each soul to expand itself in awareness such that they need not feel alone or as an island unto itself.

In karmic relationships, there is a sense of duty and obligation to others, of debts that need to be repaid, or of opportunities that one individual owes, in a sense, to another. There is also the karma or memory of the body (or the genetic self). There is the karma of the incarnational memories within each individual. There is the karma of misdeeds and misdemeanors, gifts and talents, and of contracts, covenants, and promises that need to be honored.

For karma is not to be viewed as solely negative. Karma is the great ledger in the heavens that allows balance and affords growth of each soul. It is the means by which each particular soul is monitored, assessed, and afforded the opportunities for quickening it's awareness. The intent of karma is not to focus solely on debts and obligations, but is to give inspiration and growth and allow the Divine to meet that individual soul at any level of understanding that is needed for a sense of remembrance and communion.

Karma or memory of the soul's journey makes each soul unique and special. For each soul carries the light of God consciousness within it and no soul outweighs another in the mind and the memory of the Divine.

There is much that can be found to be "wrong" in any and all individuals. But when that individual begins to truly desire to better himself, to express himself in new and better ways, then there is an outpouring of love and an outpouring of light for that self and others.

It is then that all relationships improve and all those that are touched by this one are elevated. All rise in awareness and consciousness together, not only in the earthly-framework, but in the Divine-framework as well.

For the Divine law that governs all relationships is the law of communion which transcends all contracts, debts, and obligations incurred and formed in the earth.

And this law of communion is oneness.

As each soul learns and achieves, so do all souls learn. In patience, all will come again into a state of oneness with that tremendous and wondrous force that moved so long ago and is the light within the darkness.

## THE BEGINNINGS AND ENDINGS OF ALL RELATIONSHIPS

When man looks up into a clear night sky and sees the myriad of lights that are the moons and the planets and the stars, he may be struck by the harmony, the balance, and the wonder of the universe. In the laws that guide the movements and in the pattern that guides the unfoldment, he may sense a 'spirit' and he may sense a 'purpose'.

And perhaps, just for a moment, he may reflect on his relationship with the Great Mind that wove the very patterns in the heavens.

When man looks again to the earth and can look beyond the creations that he and others have made, before him and around him are the works of Divine nature. If there is stillness, he may hear the chirp of the insects or the evening songs of the birds. He may be swept away by the sound of the wind through the trees and grasses or be lifted by the fragrances that seem to swim around him.

And perhaps, just for a moment, he may feel his relationship with the spirit and the life that is the very soul of the earth.

When man looks upon himself, lifts his hands, opens and examines them, he may sense the awe and wonder of the life that allows him to live and breathe and have his being.

And perhaps, just for a moment, he may experience his relationship with the spirit of life that is the gift and the expression of his very soul.

In gazing up at the heavens again, there may arise within him a deepening sense of humility. There may be feeling of awe and of being no more than a speck of dust or a grain of sand in comparison to the grandeur and the majesty of all of creation. So small is man...so trivial...so seemingly insignificant.

Yet, each thought, each feeling, each experience, each relationship that man has and is having, is known within the Great and Universal Mind.

In man's limited thinking and awareness, this is the most difficult aspect for him to comprehend. That the speck of dust that each man is can be important enough in the universal scheme to be made note of in the one and great mind of the Divine.

How is it possible, the body-mind of man reasons, that each and every soul can be watched, cared for, and nurtured? On earth alone there are billions and billions of souls and thousands of trillions of thoughts, feelings, and experiences each and every moment of each and every day. Tens of thousands of trillions of karmic memories that need to be blended with each man's present events with himself, the groups, and the masses through which he associates. Add to this the complexity of the soul of the earth and its needs and desires and all those in the heavens, the task is impossible.

Yet, it is truth that nothing is impossible with the Divine. No barrier is impassable. No "thing" is unachievable within the grace and the power of all that is.

There are no accidents in creation. There are no coincidences. There are no random events or such things as luck or chance.

For all that occurs to man, no matter how insignificant he may perceive it to be, is recorded and is meaningful and has within it, a Divine purpose. And each occurrence has been orchestrated in the heavens in accordance with the needs, lessons, and desires of that individual soul.

The earthly-drama of mankind is that, in each occurrence, man is free to choose whether to react from his past errors or to respond to that event in harmony with his understanding of life Divine.

In this time of transition, there will be those children of the light who choose the darkness of ignorance and desire to bear witness to the "spirit of error", just as there will be the children of the earth who choose the light of truth and bear witness to the "spirit of love". Each must bear the consequences of his decision, for life is a continuum, and this is but one event in the soul of man's journey through space and time.

Just as the soul of man began its journey in the heavens, the desire of the Divine is and has always been, that the soul of man will end its journey in the heavens, resting on the bosom and beholding and speaking with the Great One as in the beginning... face to face.

## 3.2    CHANGING INTIMATE EARTHLY RELATIONSHIPS

The beginning and the ending of all relationships, the alpha and the omega, the start and the finish, is the Divine.

Between these two, there is a song that each soul has chosen to sing, either in dischord or in harmony with the song of creation. There is a dance that each soul has chosen to dance, either in-step or out-of-step with the Lord of the Dance. There are lessons to be learned, learnings to be shared, growth to be experienced, life to be lived, and truth to be sought and tasted and felt in all the realms and all the dimensions of God's house of many mansions.

In this time of transition, the growth and change that is being experienced by the children who seek the light will profoundly impact all of their most intimate earthly or incarnational relationships.

The waves that are caused by the individual's spiritual awakening will ripple through his family, his community, and his nation, until it washes through the soul of mankind and upwards and downwards to the very gates of heaven and the very gates of hell.

In this way, all with whom that individual associates, consciously or through the resonance within the collective unconscious, will be called to change.

That is why for each earth-bound soul who becomes aware and begins to search for truth, there is great rejoicing in the heavens. For all souls are illuminated by this one candle being lit and by the one individual who becomes inflamed with the desire for light and love.

The effect of this change in each individual's spiritual awareness will either strengthen the commitment, bonding, or richness of his existing relationships or it will weaken, sever, or aid in their separation.

Why relationships are formed or broken can be found within their original purpose. And the purpose begins in the spirit of relationship that resides and is maintained in the heavens.

## SPIRITUAL COVENANTS AND EARTHLY CONTRACTS

Prior to the incarnation of each soul into the earthly-framework, that soul examines the opportunities that are given by the lights of conception that beckon to it as a means or an avenue of incarnation into the earth.

The purpose or mission of the soul is determined by that soul, in consort with the Divine, as well as the learnings and opportunities for growth that would be made available. Then there is a discussion between the souls who will play out the drama in the earth, of how each will help and aid the other.

The commitments and promises made in the heavens between souls is termed a covenant.

Unlike man wherein, in dealing with others through earthly contracts, the intent and the words that bind him to fulfill his promises are so often broken. In the heavens the covenant of a soul binds it to fulfill its promise and cannot be broken, save by the Divine.

For the covenant between souls transcends all other earthly contracts, duties, regulations, and obligations.

The Divine has covenants with the souls of mankind such that no soul shall be lost, nor any soul forgotten. The children of the light have a covenant with the Divine to illuminate the darkness and with the souls of mankind to aid in awakening them from their slumber.

In this way, souls covenant with one another. That covenant continues throughout all the ages and throughout all the dimensions until it is fully and finally fulfilled.

When a soul incarnates on the earth, it's awareness is constricted. There is a forgetfulness and a sense of limitation and separation. There is then free will that allows choice, not in knowledge as in the heavens, but often in ignorance.

This separation causes a haunting and a desire within that soul for relationship or companionship. It causes within that soul a desire for creative expression. And it causes within that soul a desire for wholeness and fulfillment.

The intimate relationships that are formed in the earth, whether within earthly family, friendships, or marriage, are mainly reflections of the covenants that were put in place before that soul's incarnation driven by these separation induced desires.

Why we say "mainly" is that sometimes the individual is so steeped in physicality that he cannot be aware of the promptings of his soul through his mind and emotions. In ignorance, he forms relationships which should not have been formed for the learning or opportunity of his soul. This too is a choice, although one made in ignorance, by that individual.

The basis for earthly relationships, then, is the desire for growth and creativity in the presence of love. There is a desire for each to be as a helpmate for that other and to allow himself to be the best he can be on the earth. But each must strive to retain and maintain an awareness of himself. For no one who desires a healthy and a healing earthly relationship should strive to manipulate or control another. No one, who desires a healthy relationship, should allow himself to be submerged or lose his sense of self in another.

What maintains earthly souls in relationship is common purpose. When that purpose changes, all aspects of the relationship must change as well. And that change will, in time, either bring these souls closer together or push them farther apart.

When the change is one precipitated from the calling of the Divine, then what may occur is one may experience growth while the other desires sameness. This becomes the dilemma in all earthly contracts. For even if individuals covenanted to aid and be as helpmates for one another through a specific incarnation, there is always free will. There is always the determinations of that soul within the earthly incarnation that can seek to lead it towards fulfillment of that covenant, or seek to lead it away.

The issue for the one who has chosen growth and life is to continue to honor the earthly contracts, duties, and obligations which they contain, or to choose to continue to grow into closer relationship with the Divine.

This too, then, becomes a free will decision by the soul who desires growth. How far will they go? Will they acknowledge self and self's relationship to the Divine, or will they submerge, suppress, and submit yet again?

The consequence of this change in spiritual growth and awareness will be a greater and greater witnessing to the truth of thoughts and emotions and, therein, a growth in that which is perceived as individualism.

The agony and the anxiety that is experienced by those souls who are attempting to respond to the calling in this time from the Divine is the impact it will have on their most intimate relationships.

There will arise fear, guilt, and self-doubt. There will be the worry and the anxiety and the trauma. They will feel that they are the cause of the rift in the relationship and take on the responsibility for the same negative emotions that are felt by those whom they have impacted. And there will be a deep sense of pain and anguish and grief in their hearts.

But beyond these feelings, there is a promise from the Divine that if one simply trusts and allows, all will be well. All will be made right if that individual is responding seriously and with sincerity to what he believes to be the call of the Divine.

## JOINING AND DIVIDING

What joins souls together, then, is spiritual purpose and the desires that arise from earthly incarnations.

The struggle that confronts those souls who are awakening to the call of the Divine is the conflict between that soul's purpose, mission, and desires and those of the earthly personality or body-mind. The lack of understanding in the body-mind of that soul is that in living and expressing its soul's purpose, all desires can be truly fulfilled.

When there is the beginning of awareness that an intimate earthly relationship is ending, that there is no longer a sense of intimacy or closeness, that there is no longer a sense of creativity, nor a feeling of growth and fulfilling expression, then there is a dividing that occurs between these two.

The division is as if the sword of truth begins to sever the spirit or purpose within the relationship, then the feelings or emotions, then their thoughts and beliefs, finally manifesting into physical expression in the earth.

When two individuals begin to grow apart in purpose, their lives begin to move in different directions. There may be a physical fulfillment of their desire for companionship, but there occurs a growing distancing and lack of closensess or intimacy. They each may begin to seek creative expression and fulfillment outside of the relationship through others or activities. They may share, but there is a lack of involvement and the sharing becomes more and more polite conversation or argument, in opposition to the deep caring and concern that may have been experienced before.

One or both may grow in awareness that something is incorrect and that something is wrong with the relationship. They may try to find means and methods of righting the sense of wrongness. When these means fail, and they so often do when the purposes of each changes, then there is a growing anger and resentment that is often suppressed by one or both.

The anger and the resentment causes an even further distancing that drives a wedge between these two in terms of mental and emotional intimacy.

And finally, the sword of truth continues its descent until the relationship manifests in some form of physical separation.

Once there is a distancing and time for reflection, the signs and omens that led up to the parting become apparent.

There are then options for the relationship. The relationship could be divided on all levels and remain so. The relationship could be reconstructed and re-entered on all levels once again. Or the relationship could be re-joined on different levels in unique and often creative ways.

## Remaining Divided

For some, this division in relationship will be accompanied by tremendous relief and feelings of freedom and expansiveness.

Many relationships wherein the sense of love is lacking should be ended or negated. For if there is not love, then there are no stirrings of the heart. In time, the heart is numbed and the doorway which could lead to the Divine is, in a sense, closed for those involved in that relationship.

If the division was appropriate (in the sense that all duties, obligations, and covenants between these two were completed) and if this releasing was completed - by at least one of the two -with love, understanding, and the knowledge that all would best be served by the separation, then there may be a parting without further need for relations in the earth again.

## Reconstruction or Re-joining

It is the desire of the Divine and all those who reside in the heavens that, when there is a sense of love, there would be a form of continuance in relationship.

Although the relationship may have ended on some levels, it could continue on others. For when the hand and the love of the Divine is present in the parting, all those impacted by the dividing, joining, or re-joining must in time and in patience, be blessed.

The form of this blessing, however, will be unique for each soul and for each soul's relationship.

In the heavens, no soul feels itself to be separate from another for there is always a sense of oneness in and through the Divine.

In this way, if in the parting there are still lessons to be learned, or covenants at a soul level to be fulfilled, then the binding in the heart or soul of these will cause them to relate again and again in new and perhaps unique ways, until all is in accordance with each soul and the Divine.

The waves of movements that bring these souls together and apart are orchestrated by the Divine for each soul's learning and understanding. These movements may seek to clarify issues that still seem to be confusing so that there is greater acceptance of the parting, or it may seek to re-establish connections on one or more levels of their beings in order to facilitate a form of reconstruction.

Each orchestration is designed so that the best may happen for all souls that will allow the creative fulfillment of their chosen purpose in the earth.

There are many paths that can lead one to this sense of spiritual and earthly wholeness, but in the scheme of God's universal and Divine plan, there is but one WAY.

And that way is through the desire and experience of LOVE DIVINE.

## DIVINE LOVE AND INTIMACY

Love is the Power and the Spirit that sustains and maintains all of creation.

Love is the Life that one may experience if he so chooses, in the earth.

Love is the Creative Expression and fulfillment of all soul's desires.

Love is the Memory of all that has transpired that makes one special and unique in the eyes of the Divine.

Love is the Peace and the Harmony that is beyond all human and earthly understanding.

Love is the Will and the desire to be of service to self, others, and the Divine.

Love is the Truth that underlies all spiritual and earthly existence.

Love is the Love for Love's sake alone.

And intimacy is the relationship that the Divine desires with all His manifestations and creations. To be close to them and to be one with them if each of those creations will allow. And for them to know that they are one with Him and still remain, uniquely themselves.

In this time when man's most intimate earthly relationships will be in an ever increasing state of change, there is one idea, one notion, one concept, and one place where one may find that which will remain stable and secure in the midst of turmoil and confusion.

And that place is the love of the Divine within.

## 3.3 DEALING with the FRUITS of TRANSITION

The changes to the individual which accompany his growing spiritual awareness will impact every area of his earthly life. These changes will move and affect his most intimate earthly relationships and flow into his work environments, community, social structures, and beyond.

The fruits of this change will be, initially, chaos and dismay that will be replaced over time, as his soul awareness emerges, into peace and profound knowingness of what should be shunned and what should be done by that soul.

Although seemingly strange, one of the many initial causes of fear in those who seek the light is the emergence in their mental, emotional, and physical natures of a sense of peace and harmony, love and hope.

For these spiritual states are so unfamiliar to those who for so long have been constricted by the pain of the heart, the churning of their bellies, and the numbness of their emotions towards self, that when they begin to feel these elevated states of consciousness they become frightened. In a sense, their body-minds yearn for those who were their friends and companions during much of their earthly sojourns, those companions that were "negativity", "hopelessness", and "pain".

In dealing with these positive fruits of transition, it will simply take some time for the children who seek the light, to become accustomed to feeling good about themselves and their tenure on the earth, rather than always desiring to escape back to their heavenly homes.

In a very real way, there will be no need for them to return to their home in the heavens, for their heavenly home is descending to meet them here in the earth.

For those who choose to remain in ignorance, there will be greater and greater instability and confusion. As the earthly-framework spins ever faster, many of these children who have chosen the earth will search for a way out of this frightening confusion and will, amongst all of their options, contemplate the taking of their earthly lives.

The taking of the gift of life is seen as a profound error or sin in the heavens. For in creation, life was given to all souls by the Divine and only the Divine has the right to remove the life of the soul from any vibrational awareness in which that soul may manifest.

The taking of one's life is a means of escape, but the better way is to escape by facing one's challenges and opportunities. To choose to escape, not into the spirit of error and the darkness of even further dismay, but into the awareness of the Divine.

At some stage of experience or unfoldment in these times of unparalleled changes, the emotions that will seek to paralyze and prevent souls from reaching heavenwards with their conscious awareness, will be fear, self-doubt, worry, and guilt.

### FEAR in the HEARTS and MINDS of MEN

Fear is the most destructive of emotional states that impedes the mental and spiritual development of mankind. It is a vibration that, along with worry, self-doubt, bitterness, and resentment, actually weighs more and is heavier than the vibrations that are associated with hope, peace, and love.

This burden and weight of these negative emotions, tends to draw the soul of man into the depths of physicality.

To walk the path of enlightenment, the soul of man must then seek to release and "let-go" of these emotions so that the burdens that he carries may be made lighter.

To release, one needs to first convert, repent, or turn-around and begin to face rather than suppress or avoid the issues that reside within. There is a need to walk through the door that is obscured by the presence of fear and negativity, and to disarm the forces of darkness that seek to maintain man's state of ignorance.

Then, the individual can truly begin to know, not merely believe and understand, but to know that life is a continuum. That the transitions that the soul experiences of life and death are merely dramas needed for soul development, and not to be feared.

When an actor begins to believe that the stage upon which he acts is his whole life, then there is a difficulty in extracting his awareness from the illusion of life that the stage creates.

The actor in the earthly drama is mortal, but the soul of that actor is immortal. The actor is born, lives on the earth, and dies, but the soul of that actor was born, and like the Divine that gave it birth, is now and forever more eternal. The actor experiences loneliness, isolation, pain, pleasure, and separation, but the soul of that actor contains the remembrance of loving oneness. The actor may feel that his life is purposeless, whereas his soul senses purposefulness in all actions, thoughts, and feelings.

In dealing, then, with the actor's illusion of fear which prevents the rise or descent of courage and strength from his soul, the actor must ask of the soul (and the Divine that resides within that soul) to aid him in overcoming his fear. The actor, personality, or body-mind of the soul must freely seek to release its fears so that they may be burned by the spirit of truth on the altars of the Divine.

In this way, each should pray and affirm to their heavenly Image of God to remove the fear that paralyzes and grips them and prevents them from acting, within the earthly drama, in accord with what they know in their heart to be true.

For one only needs to ask and it will be given. Knock, and the door will be opened. Pray with sincerity from the heart, and the Divine will aid in alleviating all your fears, turmoils, and confusion. The Divine will lift your negativity and, if you remain awake, these debilitating "states" will never return again into your awareness.

## DEALING WITH GUILT

If fear with all its children is the most destructive emotional state within man, then the most insidious is GUILT. For it is through guilt that man allows himself to be controlled and manipulated by forces that exist outside of himself.

Guilt results when an individual's thoughts, feelings, or actions are not in accord with the rules, regulations, or expectations of others. When that individual does not live up to - in his own mind - externally imposed expectations, there is guilt.

The repository and custodian of all external and internal

expectations of self in relationship to others is man's conscience. All that an individual must do and must not do to be accepted by those others with whom he associates is ingrained and contained within his conscience.

In this time of growing responsibility for self, the struggle within the individual is due, in part, to the reorienting, reforming, and the reinspiring of man's conscience with spiritual principles, values, and awareness and not simply earthly ones.

Guilt, then, is the blending of man's earthly conscience with fear and self-doubt. The fear arises from the sense within the body and mind of man of having done something wrong. Whereas the self-doubt is a not knowing in self what next to do about that sense of wrongness.

There is then a paralysis, immobility, and inability to move forward and a pain that prevents moving back. The expression of the soul into the solar-plexus area to aid in releasing the blockage is in itself blocked and the expression of man in the earth is hindered and incapacitated.

And the spirit of error delights in seeing a soul in this state of non-awareness and inability.

For the spirit of error seeks to claim for itself the souls of mankind through influencing their bodies and their minds. The most insidious means through which this error-laden spirit seeks to maintain, sustain, and contain man's soul in physicality is through the use and application of that state of mind known as guilt.

The spirit of love allows, whereas the spirit of error seeks ever to control. Love strives to always give man options and choices, whereas "error" seeks to entrap and enslave.

Love is accepting and forgiving, whereas "error" is judging and condemning. Love is giving the best that one can be whereas "error" is taking the opportunity to be the best away from each and every soul.

When the individual abdicates his responsibility for self and lives his earthly life in accordance with the expectations of others, when there is a blind acceptance with no thought or reflection on how these external standards align with that individual's personal image of god, this then becomes the true ERROR in the mind of the Divine.

When one gives more credence to what others believe they should be doing as opposed to what they are doing, what others feel they should be thinking as opposed to acknowledging what they are thinking, what others think they should be feeling as opposed to what they truly are feeling, then there is guilt and self-doubt.

These individuals then, become paralyzed and in a sense immobilized as to what they should or should not do. If they then act out of guilt rather than love, the path they walk is an ever descending spiral.

For in bearing witness to the truth of others, they are negating their own truth or personal experience and desires. The more they negate their own truth the dimmer their awareness of self becomes until, in time, there is a state of total self-negation, abdication, and confusion.

Within these individuals there is a sense of hopelessness, imprisonment, and self-sacrifice due to their continued denial of self for the sake of others. More guilt is felt, for they believe that they should not feel this way about their situation or their life, and this results in a further withdrawal from the knowledge of self and an ever growing, but so often suppressed, anger, resentment, and bitterness.

For the individual to remove himself from this descending spiral of guilt there must be FORGIVENESS, not necessarily of those others, but first and foremost of self.

Forgive yourself for all your perceived mistakes, sins, or errors, for as you do it to yourself, the Divine will allow it to be done unto you.

For how has it been given by that master soul when he was questioned how many times one should forgive? Seven times seven? Seven times seventy? Seven times seven hundred times should one forgive the self for being forgetful of the presence of the Divine within. Forgive the self for all of the perceived errors of commission or ommission.

For if one truly believes in his heart that he has sinned, then he has. For the Divine does not judge another, but the soul of man judges itself. To penetrate the guilt-induced barrier that prevents communion with your soul, you must FORGIVE and then resolve to commit that error towards self no more.

Through forgiveness of self in accord with the Divine and then the forgiveness of those others, the forgiveness and presence of the Divine will be allowed to flow into your conscious awareness.

For God forgives all souls if they would only ASK.

The life force that could not circulate due to the barrier-like presence of guilt, will then begin to flow again, bringing with it new-life and a new awareness of self's relationship to the Divine.

Through the act of forgiveness, there is an acknowledgement that sin and error does not comprise the core of your being, but rather what is present there is the light and love of the Divine.

In this Final Crusade, the armour of the Divine is virtue that is born of the acceptance and the love of self. And the sword that will clear the path towards your growing spiritual awareness is the sword of truth, a truth that is born of desiring, experiencing, and personally feeling the active presence of the Divine.

## 3.4  The LORD of the DANCE of INTIMACY

Each soul has a yearning and a longing for intimacy in relationship with self, others, and the Divine.

This spiritually induced desire for intimacy is often counterbalanced in the earth by the fear of intimacy. The interaction and reactions of this desire and this fear becomes the dance of intimacy that most individuals dance with each other during their earthly tenure.

The desire for intimacy is born within the individual with the physical incarnation of his soul in the earth. For the soul, in passing through the veil of forgetfulness, is haunted and motivated by a deep and unyielding sense of isolation. Within these individuals, there is separation, emptiness, and a feeling that there is a missing piece that they need to complete them, fulfill them, and make them whole.

As they grow and mature, they learn the rules and prescriptions - by precept and example - of how within the earthly drama one may establish the conditions that could allow them to fill their haunting emptiness.

For remember, the experiment on the earthly-framework was for the love of the Divine to be experienced through physicality in the earth. In man's evolution upwards towards the Divine, this sense of separation blended with love was to be as a motivator that would allow him to rise into Divine awareness.

But instead of seeking the Divine, most often these earthbound souls seek to create and attain the right physical and social environments, the right earthly knowledge and education, the right social, political, or administrative position, the right set of behaviours, personality, and characteristics, and the right image of self that will lure and ensnare and capture their all-elusive spectre of earthly happiness and fulfillment.

The fear of intimacy arises within the individual due to thoughts and feelings of unworthiness and self-negation. The fear establishes a belief within the heart and mind of that individual that if others truly came to know what resided at his core, then they could not or would not accept. There would then be rejection, abandonment, and all of the accompanying pain, grief, and anguish that arises from the loss of the opportunity for intimacy in the earth; an opportunity which the soul of that individual yearns for, longs for, and so hauntingly desires.

From the earliest times of growth and maturation in the earth, each individual establishes boundaries and limits of sharing and intimacy in relationship with himself and with others.

In the beginnings of intimate earthly relations, there is usually a sense of caution and a gradual movement to test the levels, strength, and tenacity of these self-established boundaries between two individuals.

If there is a determination that a type of union should occur, there is often then a releasing of some of these boundaries that is accompanied by a sense of newness, discovery, and freshness.

There is a joy that the state of love brings that creates an aura and a glow about these individuals that is recognizable and seen by others. The bonding of thought and emotions, the binding and building, and the weaving of dreams are all part of the freshness and the experience of a new-born relationship.

As the spirit of the relationship matures, and dependent on the purposes of each, there is a type of physical, mental, emotional, and spiritual balance reached between their earthly roles and responsibilities, the elements that comprise their relationship, and each other.

This balance or comfort zone is determined by the desire for intimacy on the one hand with the fear of intimacy on the other.

When the desire for intimacy of one individual grows and that one attempts to move closer, on some level, to the other, most often what occurs is that the other moves away in order to maintain and preserve the balance.

Then there begins the dance of earthly intimacy.

One may feel a sense of rejection and the other may feel limited and constrained. The one will withdraw or may become angry while the other will feel misunderstood and unappreciated. There may be condemnation, judgement, and criticism and there results an even further withdrawal by one or the other or both.

When the distance exceeds the limits of intimacy that were in place before the movement began, then what follows is the growth in the fear of the loss of intimacy. This fear of loss, which is so often associated with guilt, then motivates a type of reconciliation and a re-establishment of what had been before.

The result is a sense of frustration, a lack of growth, a lack of movement, with the consequent lack of meaningful change in either the relationship or the individuals within that relationship.

And when the desire for intimacy grows in one or the other of the two, the dance begins yet again with often the same unfulfilling results.

Unless there is the intrusion of an internal or external force that impacts the relationship, it may continue in a lack of creative expression, lack of fulfillment, and a continuing sense of dissatisfying sameness.

In this time of transition, the internal force that is serving to change intimate earthly relationships is the calling of the Divine from the heavens.

The external force that is seeking to change intimate earthly relations is the compression of time and the impacting of the political, socio-economic, and earth changes that will surround and affect all souls with ever increasing frequency as the decade progresses.

To prepare oneself for these changes in earthly relationships, either for rejuvenating existing intimate relationships or forming new intimate unions, the fear of intimacy must be overcome.

## OVERCOMING OUR FEAR OF INTIMACY

The image of self is the chief obstacle that prevents the experience of intimacy in the earth.

There are many children who are both unfirm and infirm about who and what and why they are. This negation of self and self's desires and their continuing abdication of self-responsibility leads to a sickness and a lack of stability.

Intimacy cannot occur, either in the earth or with the

Divine, unless there is a firmness in the understanding of the true nature of the self. For without this firmness in this image of the true self, there arises a fear of the loss of self when entering into potentially intimate relationships.

The fear of the loss of self is created and preserved by the body-mind, ego, or personality in consort with the karmic body-mind or the store-house of man's earthly incarnational memories. The body-mind is charged with the creation of the earthly self while the solar-plexus or karmic body-mind, is charged with preserving the earthly self.

When the boundaries that appeared mentally and emotionally comfortable are penetrated by another in an attempt at intimacy, there is then a reaction of fear.

And the most intimate of all relationships is the one that is sought with the Divine, and in turn, the Divine will seek to penetrate all of your barriers and boundaries in order to awaken you to His presence.

The image of spiritual emergence that often confounds the seekers on the path is one of the drop of water (that is their soul), merging with the ocean (that is the Divine). The feelings associated with this image is the total loss of self or a kind of spiritual death.

There is an aspect of truth in this image for the ascent and awakening of the crown chakra does allow the soul to leave and find oneness with All That Is.

But at the same time as the soul is moving into the awareness of the Divine, the Divine is moving into the very body of the soul. In this way, the son that is the soul of man moves towards the Father, and the Father moves towards the son. The drop of water moves into the ocean, and the ocean descends and moves into the drop of water.

For the purpose and fulfillment of man's earthly existence is not just to know oneness with the Divine, for the soul of mankind knew that oneness in the very beginning. The purpose and fulfillment for man's soul is to know itself to be itself and yet one with the Divine.

But to reach this state of knowingness, there must be a releasing, surrender, or letting-go of earthly negativity. It is a releasing of all of your fears, worrys, doubts, and confusion. It is a letting-go of all aspects of your earthly nature that obscures the beauty of your own soul. It is surrendering the right to be confused, ignorant, and poor in spirit. Then your true self will be allowed to emerge, express, and ascend, for to enter the kingdom of heaven, individuals must first clean their feet of clay.

In this way, the fear of the loss of self is but another trick or illusion that seeks to maintain mankind in his state of inner darkness.

For in truth, by continually striving to experience the most intimate of all relationships with the Creator and the Maker of all things, you will not lose yourself, but rather you will find yourself once more.

And once you experience the great love of all the universes, your fear of intimacy will dissolve and you will have the freedom in knowledge to choose to fulfill your desire for intimacy in the earth.

## ATTRACTING HEAVENLY INTIMACY
## INTO THE EARTH

There is much truth that each individual must seek to create the appropriate conditions that will allow intimacy to occur. Mankind's confusion, however, is that he seeks to create those conditions without and neglects to strive to create them within.

For the presence and the very fragrance of the soul who seeks love for love's sake alone is like no other. The beauty and the grace emitted by these loving ones does not emerge from their earthly image, nor from their status and position, but from the very light of their soul that shines from within.

There is a sincerity and a humility that allows these seekers of the light to see the truth in the least and the greatest of men. There is a joy and a lightness that envelopes and surrounds them such that, by their very presence, they bring illumination to those who gather around. There is a sense of allowing in the presence of these loving ones such that others can be themselves without fear of recrimination, reproach, judgement, or condemnation.

In the presence of wrath, they offer words of kindness and reconciliation. In the face of hatred and rage, they smile and offer their peace and their equanimity. In the midst of chaos and confusion, they offer the gifts of wisdom and harmony.

These are the ways that will allow love Divine to manifest in the earth, and through these loving ones who allow themselves to be instruments of the Divine, much goodness and grace can be brought into the very soul of mankind.

If these inner conditions are nurtured, cultivated, and allowed to manifest, through them will you attract that special other who will bring you companionship, creativity, and fulfillment while on the earth; that soul mate, or brother-sister soul, or that perfect complement for which your heart yearns.

But it is in first seeking the love of the Divine for love's sake alone that will aid you in recognizing that other. It is in striving to respond in accord with your image of the Divine to all those you meet, that will attract to you that special other.

Remember always that the Great One will help to prepare you. The Great One will feed and nurture you. The Great One will teach and guide you so that you are aware and ready for that special other to come into your earthly life and, if you so choose, to become your earthly love.

For in Him, all of your earthly desires may be fulfilled. In Him, you may be made whole again. Then and only then may you be granted and allow yourself to accept the gifts of harmony, love, and joy in the earth for forever and a day.

The lord of the dance of heavenly intimacy is the Divine and the law that will bring this understanding into man's conscious awareness is not the laws of the earth, nor the laws of the mind, but the law of love in oneness Divine.

## 3.5 The TRIANGLE of LOVE

The image of love that most closely reflects that of love Divine in the earthly-framework is the image of the sun. The sun is the source of light, warmth, and energy that falls upon and sustains all of the earthly creations as does the light, warmth, and love of the one true source.

There are no favorites or special places where the sun will shed its light, just as the love of the Divine holds no favorites, but loves all souls with a love that is the same. The sun is totally giving of itself for the sake of others as is the power and love of the Divine.

The sun does not judge on whom, where, or what its life giving light should fall. It does not withold itself from some and give itself to others in a random and precocious way, but is constant, consistent, and purposeful in the fulfillment of its covenant with mankind and the Divine. In this same way, the Divine laws are as the sun in that they are constant and consistent and purposeful in their maintaining and sustaining of the Divine's covenants with all who sing in His song of creation.

The sun is a sphere that appears to have no beginning and no end for one can travel many paths upon its surface and each path can bring one back to where one began. The Divine has no beginning and has no end. Each creation may take many paths to experience the many faces and facets of the Divine, but all paths will lead back to the beginning of All That Is.

The sun is a symbol of wholeness and perfection whose light is emitted from within. And the Divine is wholeness and perfection whose light, love, and illumination come from within.

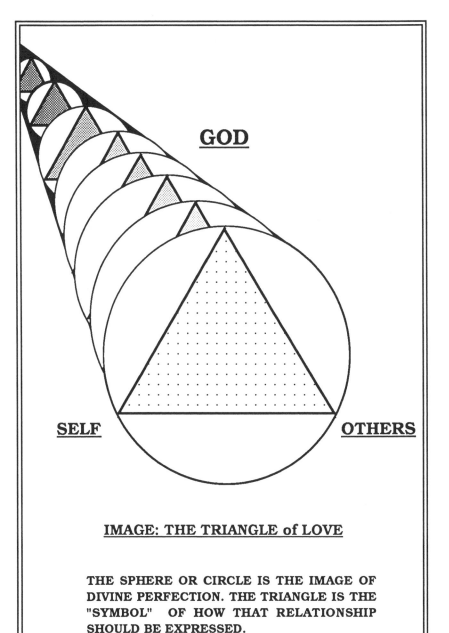

**IMAGE: THE TRIANGLE of LOVE**

THE SPHERE OR CIRCLE IS THE IMAGE OF
DIVINE PERFECTION. THE TRIANGLE IS THE
"SYMBOL" OF HOW THAT RELATIONSHIP
SHOULD BE EXPRESSED.

From the earth, the sun is seen as a circle or wheel that revolves and draws an arc across the heavens. The Divine is also seen as a circle or a wheel that, in time and in patience, will revolve and evolve all souls back to the one true source.

And man was made in the Image of God and his soul can be as the sun in the earth.

Within this sphere and within this circle that is the image of wholeness and perfection, there can be placed a triangle whose sides are all equal in length. This would then be the image of the relationship with the Divine that expresses as a ray emanating from and involving itself in, the earthly-framework.

At the pinnacle or the peak of this triangle rests God or the Divine and on each corner of the base of the foundation is SELF and OTHERS.

This would be the image that is the triangle of love for it is balance and harmony. No aspect of the triangle is more important than another. The love of the Divine has no favorites in that it falls equally on self and those others. The very foundations of the power of God's love in the earth is through the co-creative expressions, vibrations, or souls of men.

This is not the only way that God may manifest in the earth, but the spirit within the souls of men form the foundations of that Divine and co-creative expression.

### RELATIONSHIP WITHIN THE HEARTS OF MEN

Within man's heart is contained and is the means through which the spirit of love may manifest in the earth.

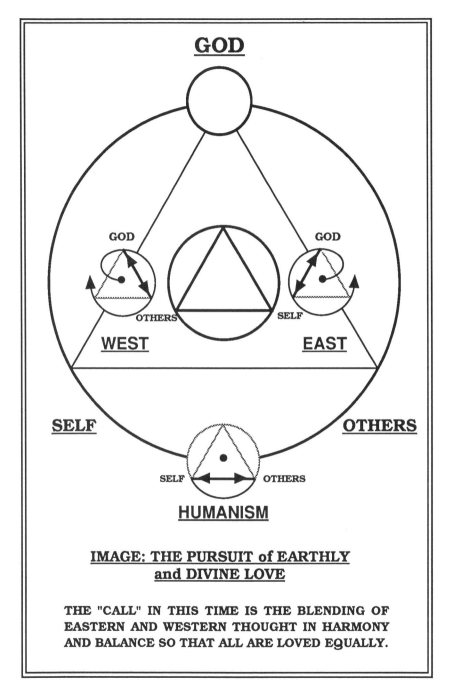

GOD

GOD

GOD

OTHERS

SELF

**WEST**

**EAST**

**SELF**

**OTHERS**

SELF

OTHERS

**HUMANISM**

## IMAGE: THE PURSUIT of EARTHLY and DIVINE LOVE

THE "CALL" IN THIS TIME IS THE BLENDING OF EASTERN AND WESTERN THOUGHT IN HARMONY AND BALANCE SO THAT ALL ARE LOVED EQUALLY.

Therein resides the love of self, the love of others, and the love of the Divine.

In the earth, if an individual loves himself and others to the exclusion of the Divine, then the result is a type of humanism. The individual is governed by what the group, community, or society believes is acceptable behaviour. There are codes of conduct, morals, ethics, dogmas, and doctrines which emerge and are molded by culture and society. Their behaviour is often situational, in that one type of behaviour may be acceptable in one situation while another is acceptable and considered normal, in another. The spiritual error that often accompanies this thought is the absence of the seeking of the truth and love of the Divine.

If an individual loves the Divine and self to the exclusion of others, then self-development takes precedence over service to others. The eastern or oriental philosophies contain and embody this type of thought wherein the seeking of the truth is found by moving within. The spiritual error that often arises within this thought is an imbalance towards self, not selfishness, but self and the Divine above all else. This thought manifests in a type of neglect and negation of man's external material needs in the earth.

If an individual loves the Divine and others to the exclusion of self, then service to others takes precedence over the concern and care of the self. The western or occidental philosophies and cultures embody this type of thought wherein the seeking of the truth is found to be external. The error that often arises in man's spiritual development is that in giving service to others he often neglects, denys, and sacrifices himself. And this thought manifests in the earth as an emphasis on man's material needs and comforts with the advancement and development of science and technology.

## THE CALL TO A NEW HARMONY

In this time, there is a call for a new harmony to manifest in the earth. A new balance between the east and the west, the inner and the outer, and that which can be found to exist within and that which can be found to exist without.

There is a need in the earth for a sense of balance such that one aspect of this triangle of love does not outweigh any other.

For if one loves his family and his friends more than himself or the Divine, that one is not worthy of the Divine. If one loves himself and the Divine more than others, than that one also is not worthy of the Divine. All must love as the sun, with equality and harmony and without partiality and dischord.

All must be loved the same. Enemies the same as friends. Family the same as non-family. Others as you would love yourself and the Divine as you would love others.

Those who have prepared themselves for this time through self-development and a movement within for the truth, are called now to move beyond themselves and take on the yoke of service to others.

In response to this calling, there is a movement beginning in the East of those known as spiritual masters, teachers, and enlightened ones who are readying themselves to move beyond the mountain hermitages and places of earthly and spiritual isolation, to emerge and begin to publicly minister to mankind in this time of transition.

Those who have developed their truth through service to others, are being called to look within and re-establish their relationship to the Divine. For the power of truth and love of the Divine can be found in others, but can also be found within.

To this end, there has been a blending of eastern thought, since the time of the industrial revolution, with western thought. It is a blending such that the "tools" that one would need to find the Divine within are present and available to all those who seek.

Regardless of which path each must walk for harmony in the earth to be achieved, there must be a remembrance in man's consciousness that God is first and foremost, then there follows self then others, or others then self.

For the law was given that,

**Thou shalt love the Lord thy God with all thy heart, mind, and soul, and thy neighbor as thyself.**

And who is thy neighbor, friend, or family? Those who strive to do the will of the Divine and act in loving accordance with their soul's purpose and desires.

The spark of the Divine resides in all souls that walk upon the earth, and the Divine can be seen within them if one's eyes are attuned to virtue and truth. Whether it is love, faith, hope, peace, or trust it can be seen to manifest without and it can also be found to reside within.

For how can one say that he loves the Divine and others, but cannot love himself? How can one say he loves the Divine and himself, but not others? And in turn, how can one say he trusts the Divine and not himself or others?

How can one say he forgive others, but cannot forgive himself? How can one say that he accepts others, but cannot bear to accept himself?

For all are ONE, and all of the many forms of duality in this present cycle of learning must be brought and blended together to invoke and evoke the presence of a NEW HARMONY in the earth.

## 3.6 The SEARCH for SOUL FAMILY

The continuing alignment and attunement of the children who seek the light will first manifest as a closer and more intimate relationship with the Divine.

These children will begin to experience more and more of the Divine reality in the form of dreams, visions, and tangible guidance. There will be heard the still small voice of the Divine within their hearts and minds and there will be felt urgings and promptings and the stirrings of their emotional selves in new and loving ways. There will be a growing awareness of their soul's purpose and they will sense more purpose and meaning behind the events and circumstances they face in their earthly lives. And there will be a growing trust that they are being nurtured, cared for, and moved by the loving hand and live under the watchful eyes of all that is.

This ongoing and growing alignment and attunement of the individual is not only with the heavens, but it is also an alignment and attunement with the Divine in the earth.

For man often forgets that the earth, as well, is a living organsim that possesses a spirit, awareness, and a body. In this time of transition, the soul of the earth is also evolving into closer relationship with the Divine. It too, has been prepared and awakened for the cleansing of karmic memories and associations that have impeded its growth and fulfillment and journey into higher awareness.

The soul of the earth is aware that its body and mind must be cleansed and purged of all the darkness and barriers that have prevented it from moving higher. It too, is aware that it must experience a break and fragmentation to be realigned and reassembled in a different way with the Divine. There is a sense within the mountains and the valleys, the waters and the airs, and the fish, fowl, and animals of the earth, that there is to be a change. And all those vibrations that comprise the soul of the earth, wait in anxious expectancy for this change to manifest.

The alignment, then, that is occurring to each individual who walks the path of enlightenment, is one that moves and stretches him upwards to the very core of the spirit of the Divine in the heavens and downwards to the very core of the spirit of the Divine in the earth.

The attunement and awakening of each individual into relationship with the Divine also carries with it, then, a sense of responsibility and obligation to help the spirit or soul of the earth fulfill its purpose of maintaining and sustaining all earthly life in love and in harmony.

As the children experience more and more of their spiritual emergence, they will come to terms, in a sense, and reach a more harmonious understanding of their place, with the Divine in the heavens, the Divine in the earth, and their most intimate earthly relationships, vocations, and earthly communities.

And there will arise an urge to find and to experience spiritual community or soul family within the earth.

When an individual meets another of the same spiritual community or soul family - and be aware that no meeting occurs by chance - then there is almost an instantaneous recognition of that other at a soul level. Depending on the degree of awareness, this recognition may be of the light of another soul through the spiritual eye, or it could be a feeling of the heart.

There is a sense of affiliation, attachment, and a flow of mutual and reciprocal sharing. Through dialogues and discussions, there would be a sense that both are on the same wavelength in thought and each will feel an almost immediate bonding, attachment, and haunting sense of remembrance. Even if the meeting was brief, each will often think about that other and try to put in place the feeling of familiarity and inexplicable intimacy.

As members of the same soul family begin to recognize, identify, and gather with one another in the earth, there is a growth and a movement in mutual development which, once begun, will not stop.

For in their meetings and sharings, there is an evolution of strength and concentration of purpose that acts like a magnet that attracts and draws others of similar thought and purpose to them. As others are drawn into these gatherings, there is then an even greater concentration of learning through the resulting collective awareness and resonance so that all begin to aid each other in alignment and attunement with the Divine.

This growing nuclear and magnetic attraction will impact all members of that soul family, whether or not they are in communication or consciously aware. On some level of their beings, all members of that spiritual community are connected and will be impacted.

This affinity is not exclusive to those soul family members who are incarnate, for in the ethers, those members who have chosen not to incarnate in this time of tribulation will also be drawn into those gatherings and be a part of their collective awareness and strive to help in the realignment of their soul families with Divine purpose and intent.

In turn, these gatherings of the children who seek the light will help to align and attune the very soul of mankind into a more intimate relationship with the Divine.

The loneliness, isolation, and separation that was a part of the motivation that led to the pursuit of truth and the seeking of the Divine, will give way to a deeper sense of acceptance, purpose, belonging and communion in the earth.

There will be much joy, growth, and harmony in this ever growing re-union of souls. As these individuals allow a greater alignment with their soul, the earth, and a sense of heavenly intimacy in their earthly relationships, as these individuals allow a greater portion of the Divine to express through them into the earth, so are all given the benefit and the blessing of that relationship, for ALL are indeed ONE.

# The CALL to a NEW APPLICATION of TRUTH

## 4.1 DIVINE LAWS and UNIVERSAL PRINCIPLES

Before the beginning, Divine and universal laws existed in the mind of the Divine. These laws were intimately associated with the light of illumination, the all-knowing and expectant darkness, and the possibilities of the movement and blending of the light and the darkness in the Divine song of creation and evolution.

In response to the desire of the First Cause, the light of truth began to expand from within the core of the Divine. Each emanating ray or vibration embodied and carried with it and within it, an awareness of its purpose and plan of unfoldment, as well as the Divine law that would govern and guide its manifestation.

The Divine laws, then, form the very framework through which each vibration can manifest its portion of the song of creation and through which it may seek to fulfill its purpose of growing into greater and greater awareness and relationship with the First Cause.

These laws can be seen as the word that flowed from the mouth of the holy of holies, and in and through its movement, became an edict, commandment, or universal law. They are consistent, immutable, unchanging, and dependable for all are aspects and facets of the one true source.

To guard and guide their manifestation and application and to ensure that the message, word, or law was the same for all the universes and all the dimensions, these laws were given over into the hands of the messengers and stewards of the First Cause. Each law or grouping of laws, has then an overseer or an angel that acts as a custodian of the word of the Divine.

The earthly-framework exists and is defined by seven rays or vibrations. All that does and can ever occur to the soul of mankind while in the earth, occurs within an aspect of these seven states of awareness.

Each vibration - and each Divine law contained within it - forms the boundaries, stage, or "playing field" wherein the "game of life" and the earthly drama can be enacted.

These Divine laws, unlike man's laws, cannot be changed nor can they be amended, avoided, or circumvented. To overcome them, man must, in a sense, become one with them, understand and fulfill them, before he can move towards a higher awareness and a deeper understanding of his true nature.

By working in harmony with these Divine laws, man can bring clarity, insight, and illumination into his mind and his heart. But by working - either in ignorance or in knowledge - against them or out of accord with these same, the fruits of his thoughts and actions must be chaos, confusion, and uncertainty.

For each individual, through the exercising of his free will in the choices made each and every moment of each and every day of earthly existence, operating and acting through these Divine laws, creates his own destiny and shapes the nature of his future events, circumstances, and relationships.

## THE DIVINE LAWS OUTSIDE OF MAN

The truth of the Divine can be found outside of man and it can also be found to reside within him.

Outside man, this search for truth is embodied in his pursuit and development of science and technology. Man, in his earthly sojourns, has evolved in his knowledge, understanding, and application of the seven divine laws and the seven vibrations of which the earth is comprised.

For remember, these laws existed from the beginning. They operate and are ever-present whether man is consciously aware of them or not. And it was as the mind of man grew in consciousness that he became more and more aware of their existence and began to use them to satisfy his earthly needs and desires.

In this day, man can gain a sense of the interactions and interrelationships of these seven universal principles as they manifest as nature within the earth.

If man stills and attunes himself while in the midst of nature, he can sense the hum and the presence of life. There is a movement of the insects and the birds, the animals and the plant life, the fungi and the grasses, the trees and the waters that, when combined, evoke a sense of harmony.

For if the harmony was not present, then this system and interrelationship would dissolve and a new balance would evolve into being, and in this way there is continual growth and creativity.

For each system, and for each element within that system, there is a cause that has produced the effect that his carnal eyes can now perceive. There is a sense of continuity and memory within this place and within this time, of something being produced and reproducing and within all the relationships of predators and their victims, between the predators and their prey, between the apparent inanimate and the animate, there is a whole that is perceived to be greater than the analysis and the addition of each of its parts.

Within that wholeness there is a feeling of truth, a sense of giving and accepting in love, and an underlying oneness.

In man's pursuit of knowledge and seeking of the truth of his earthly existence, he has often sterilized, disinfected, and divorced the spirit from the systems and the objects of his studies.

The earth, rather than being dealt with as a living organism, is treated as a thing to be exploited. The mystic sciences that linked man with nature have been washed clean of any relationship with man or the Divine in the name of objectivity and rational thought. The language so often spoken is one of numbers and mathamatics. The rhythm and the heartbeat of the spirit of the Divine is reduced to frequency and beats per fractions of seconds. And the manifestations of the Divine are overshadowed by the works and endeavors of man's pursuit of his own interests.

For man cannot seem to perceive the Divine in electricity or know the nature of its being, but he can formulate the laws and construct the equipment and establish the conditions that will allow him to use that facet of the Divine.

Man may not understand the essence of life, but through his understanding and application of the laws of life he can manipulate, rearrange, and modify the way in which that life manifests.

Man may not understand the source and nature of the energy that exists within the atoms, but through his understanding of chemical, biological, or nuclear interactions, and his application and use of the laws that govern those same, this energy can be unleashed to bring light and warmth or darkness and destruction into man's earthly experience.

Within each facet of man's earthly pursuit of the truth, man is caught in a sense of duality. Whether that duality is the physicist's search for the theory that will unify the nuclear and gravitational forces or whether it is the mystic's search for the way that will unify the forces of truth and expectant darkness, the search and the seeking is the same.

For this search is the search for oneness, which can be found to be without and can also be found to be within.

## DIVINE LAWS WITHIN THE BODY OF MAN

From the very beginning, the laws of the Divine were written into man's body, mind, and soul. These laws are found to be in association and intimate relationship with the seven dimensions, centers, or vibrations that exist within the very being of man as he expresses in the earthly-framework.

In man's three dimensional awarenesss, these laws appear to express in three distinct groupings or ways;

physical laws, mental laws, and spiritual laws.

The three-dimensional physical plane or universe can be said to be limited by time and space and it is only through patience that man may come to understand the meaning of his earthly existence. The barrier and limitation can be said to be the speed of light. For those vibrations that vibrate faster than the speed of light would belong to the realms and dimensions of thought.

The mental dimensions or realms of thought and the forms of those same, transcend all space and time limitations that are experienced by man in physicality.

For if an individual would simply stop and think, he could recall and - depending on his state of mind - re-experience in intimate detail the thoughts, feelings, and events of an earlier episode in his childhood. In this same way, that individual could, in a sense, move forward in time through a vision or a dream and apprehend and experience an event that is precognitive and has not as yet manifested in the earth.

Each individual exists, then, in a sea of thought and either adds to this sea or receives from it. This dual nature of man's mind can be best described as creative and receptive, attractive or repulsive, constructive or destructive. And where man chooses to swim in this sea of thought is dependent on what and to whom he attunes and aligns his conscious awareness.

Ideas, images, feelings, and imaginings are the way man senses the presence of these mental realms. And man senses the spiritual realms as the purpose, spirit, or motivation that stands behind the images, feelings, or earthly action.

## IMAGE: THE EVOLUTION of the "SPIRIT of LIFE"

### EVOLUTION of SPIRIT

| DIVINE LAW | | | | | | | | |
|---|---|---|---|---|---|---|---|---|
| **LOVE**<br>LIFE IN LOVE | Love For Love Sake | Wisdom In Love | Fulfill-ment In Oneness | Peace In Love | Loving Co-Creativity | Loving Memory Of All | New Life In Love | |
| **TRUTH**<br>LIFE IN TRUTH | Freedom In Truth | Desire For Love In Truth | Know-ledge In Truth | Creative Being | Spirit Memory | New Life In Truth | | |
| **DESIRE**<br>LIFE IN SPIRIT | Desire For Soul Will | Desire For Faith | Creative Spirit | Soul Memory | New Life In Spirit | | | |
| **HARMONY**<br>LIFE IN EARTHLY BALANCE | Peace Of The Earth | Purpose Full Creativity | Aware Memory | Life In Earthly Love | | | | |
| **CAUSE and EFFECT**<br>LIFE THROUGH MEMORY | Memory Of Creativity | Life In Memory | Life In Commun-ity | | | | | |
| **CREATIVITY**<br>LIFE AS CREATIVE EXPRESSION | Creativity Thru Life | Life In Family | | | | | | |
| **LIFE**<br>LIFE IN THE EARTH | Life In Self | | | | | | | |

The spirit or sense of purpose, then, becomes the manifestation of spiritual law into man's awareness and into the earthly-framework wherein he resides.

When the soul's awareness was differentiated into seven vibrations, the one law was also differentiated and formed a sense of hierarchy within the understanding of man, such that the physical laws are overcome by man's movement towards and use of the laws of the mind, and the mental laws are overcome by man's movement towards and use of the laws of the spirit.

Man's next evolutionary step is moving him from the third to the fourth dimensional state of awareness or from the depths of physicality to a richer and heightened understanding of spirituality.

In this sense, the first law that man's consciousness encounters in his soul's entry into the earth is the law of life.

### The Law of Life

**"The Divine has willed that man may
Hold in his palms and
Mold with his hands,
The gift and the spirit of LIFE"**

Written within the first chakra, center, or vibration is the law of life. Through this law man is given the ability and the right to exist separate from the First Cause and allowed to grow into a relationship with that same.

The manifestation of this law is man's physical body. It is within his breath and the vitality that respiration brings. It is within his blood and the sustenance and the cleansing that the circulation brings. It is within all those bodily systems that maintain and sustain the spirit of life within man's physical earthly existence.

Through this law of life, aligning with the gravity chakra, man is drawn into physical earthly existence and forms intimate relationships with the vibrations of the earthly soils, waters, airs, plants, and animal life and feels one and part of that same. In this way, the spirit of life is felt through the pulsing of man's heart, the rhythm of his breath, and through his mutual co-existence with those earthly vibrations and the natural laws that govern them.

The law of life is satisfied through man's gathering and partaking of water, food, warmth, and shelter. However, the fulfillment of the law of life in the earth comes from man's desire to share his life and existence with others of his own kind.

### The Law of Creativity

**"I come to give you life so that each
of you may live it more abundantly
and more creatively"**

**"And the mountains and the waters
wait in silent expectation for the
Divine plan to unfold"**

The second center or vibration has within it the law of creativity. This law governs man's ability to reproduce himself and to manifest in creative ways in the earth.

Through the working of the law within this center, man can enter into awareness of familial type relationships and, in a sense, go beyond himself and his relationship with the earth.

Through this law, there is a blending between the body and the body-mind of man such that there is an ability to reason and to analyse situations which are encountered in the earth. Through this law there is the desire for survival of the self and others with whom that self is in intimate relations.

But this law of creativity can also be said to be "like begets like" and is a law that applies in the physical as well as the mental, emotional, and spiritual realms.

In the mental and emotional realms, this desire to reproduce oneself manifests as habitual patterns of thoughts, feelings, and desires that seek to maintain man in a sense of repetitive sameness.

If, through man's determinations or the promptings of his soul, his desire for creativity grows, then man may express himself in new and different ways through the use of this law and begin to reproduce and form patterns, attitudes, and feelings of growth and expansiveness.

This law of creativity or "like begets like" also applies to the spiritual realms, for in the beginning, all souls were made in the likeness and the image of God. And the desire of the Divine is for His creations to become more like Him in co-creative expression.

The satisfying of this law can occur physically, through establishing relations in the earth and producing offspring who are made in the image of self. It can be satisfied mentally, by the creation and the maintenance of a physical environment and a mental attitude of relative comfort, security, stability, and sameness.

However, the fulfillment of this law of creativity comes from creatively expressing the gift of life in new and refreshingly different ways. For the Divine delights in the infinite variety of manifestations of his creations and desires that all souls should express in accord with their own specialness and in alignment with their own uniqueness.

This desire for growth and creativity leads the individual, in a sense, upwards to meet more and more aspects of himself through the law of cause and effect.

### The Law of Cause and Effect

**"Knock and the door will be opened, seek and you will find."**

**"Come all those who are heavy laden, and I will give you rest."**

The third center or vibration contains within it the law of cause and effect. The solar-plexus is the center of man's earthly power and is the place through which man reacts to earthly situations in emotional ways.

In the earth, this law manifests as an awareness that for each and every *cause* there is a form of *effect*. For each and every *action*, there is some form of *reaction*. And for each and every *movement*, there is a corresponding *counter-movement*.

In the mind, this law manifests as memory or remembrance. It is not just the memory of man's current incarnation, but is also the memory of *all* incarnations of that soul within the earthly-framework that can be accessed through this third center.

In the spirit, this law manifests as soul memory that contains all the manifestations of the soul in all dimensions and all the universes. This "book of life" is stored within God's hall of records that is within the memory and the mind of the Divine.

The soul record is used to monitor each soul's progress either towards or away from the Divine and determines the challenges, lessons, and opportunities required by and for each earth-bound soul.

The purpose or the spirit behind this law of cause and effect is the preservation of the self, self's relationship with the earth, self's relationship with others, and self's relationship with the Divine. There is a sense of continuity and continuance in the actions and operations of this law that causes man to react to preserve himself.

In physically threatening situations, there is a reaction of fear that causes the individual to fight or flee. In mentally threatening situations that are perceived as harmful to his self-image, there may be a reaction of fear, worry, anger, or withdrawal. And all of the individual's reactions, on every level of his being, are faithfully and unerringly recorded.

The desires that arise from this center may compel man to preserve his earthly identity through familial or community associations, making a "mark" in some way within the records of humanity, or through the building of edifices, monuments, and a variety of tangible earthly creations.

Another aspect of this law of karma or cause and effect is that through the workings and operation of this law, man meets every aspect of himself. The fruits and the harvest of events and experiences, throughout man's earthly sojourn, are the product of his purposes, thoughts, feelings, and actions that he "planted" (within himself) in the recent or distant past.

The cause, then, of man's present earthly experience (or effects) are the determinations man has made in the past. What brings man's future experiences to him are the reactions, responses, or choices he is making today.

What is important about man's determinations is whether he chooses to "react" from old and often limited ways or "responds" to life in new and creative ways. Whichever choice man makes, it is neither the thought nor the action which follows that determines whether a soul gains or loses on the path toward his Maker, but the purpose or intent that stands behind his thoughts and his actions.

In each earthly event, man is free to choose his reactions or responses to that event. And even the Divine does not know the outcome until man's choice is made. Once made, however, the law of cause and effect moves, records, and serves to bring back to that individual another challenge or opportunity for growth.

What may be confusing (in man's understanding) is that some earthly events seem pre-determined and can be predicted and prophecized prior to their earthly manifestation. This phenomenon can be better understood through the recognition of the force or condition that occurs with the alignment of man's four-fold nature.

When the spirit or *purpose, thought* and belief, feelings and *desires*, and man's goals and *actions* are in alignment and accord, then that condition must manifest in the earth in time. This is true for the individual and is also true for mankind.

Those who have prepared themselves and consciously attune to these seed-thoughts and images that reside in man's collective sea of thought or move their awareness into the spiritual realms and sense the purpose or intent of that condition and determination, can then apprehend - in the form of prophetic visions, etheric voice, or pre-cognitive dreams and images - these impending events before they impact the earth.

The satisfying of this law of cause and effect is in the meeting of self on every level of being, physically, mentally, or spiritually to whatever degree necessary for the scales of justice or the great ledger in the heavens to be balanced. In this way, all will discharge their debts, duties, and obligations or reap their rewards of talents, abilities, and gifts in the course of earthly incarnation.

However, the fulfillment of this law occurs through the desire to seek a better way, to escape from this wheel of earthly life, and to look for the truth and love of the Divine.

And in this way, through manifesting the gift of life as strength, courage, and perseverence in his search for "love", the individual may move upwards from the memories of karma to the harmonies of grace.

### The Law of Harmony

**"I come to give you peace, a peace
that surpasses all earthly understanding"**

The fourth center or the heart chakra is the custodian of the law of harmony. The heart is the great crossroads between the forces of man's spiritual nature and the forces of man's earthly nature and it is only in harmony that these two can be blended in the conscious awareness of mankind.

In the earth, this law manifests as balance. Unlike the balance of justice that lies below it in the realms and dimensions of karma, this is the balance that is weighed in love. For often love does not appear just in the eyes and the judgements of man, but it is just and pleasing in the eyes of the Divine.

Harmony can be seen within the movements of the stars

and within movements of the atom, for the forces of attraction, that are seen as gravity in the earth, are balanced by the forces of repulsion that allow form and substance to exist within God's song of creation.

The heart of man was set within him to draw him towards the heavens, just as the gravity chakra seeks and endeavors to draw him into the physicality of the earth. The heart is the opposite pole to physicality that conforms to the original designs and desires of the Divine for man's expression in the earth.

Harmony is then the levity that lifts man from the weight of the mediocre and mundane and puts to rest the endless spinning of man's wheel-of-life and earthly drama. There is peace in harmony and the heart of man is the great peacemaker within his being.

The principle that works in and through the law of harmony is love. For man will sacrifice his earthly life for the sake of love. Man will relinquish his right to reproduce himself in the earth for the sake of love. Man will give up his expressions of creativity and risk imprisonment and suffering in the name of love. Man will pay all his debts, service all his duties, give all he has preserved and felt himself to be for the sake and in the name of love.

It is through love that harmony can enter man's conscious awareness and bring with it new life. For if a man gives his earthly life for another in the name of love, he will be given his soul-life from the heavens. The sacrifice of the darker and negative aspects of the earthly-self for the sake of love Divine, is what is being asked of each and every soul that exists on the face of planet earth in this time of transition.

The heart of man, however, is often numbed and in pain from the hurt and misuse and abuse accorded to it through its earthly incarnations. The way to awaken the heart, then, is through love. For the heart always responds to love. Like a hungry child who seeks nurturing from his mother, the heart and soul of man responds to the nurturing vibrations of love.

Through love, man awakens to a new understanding and awareness of his earthly existence. Most often, the individual will awaken first to love through others in intimate earthly relationship, and then will be faced with a choice whether to remain in earthly relationship alone, or move beyond into the searching and the seeking for love Divine.

For the law of harmony marks a path that ascends into the heavens, but can also be walked in descent back into the earth. From the heart, man can look down towards his physicality or he can look up towards his spirituality. There can be found a sense of peace in earthly relationships alone, but the peace that passes all human understanding can only be found in the ascent of man's awareness towards his spiritual nature.

The law of harmony can also be said to be "like attracts like". For whatever man holds in his heart in thoughts, beliefs, feelings, and desires is what he becomes through the operation of this law of attraction. The personality or body-mind may desire, think, and strive to do, but the beliefs held within his heart may negate and frustrate all his earthly efforts.

All men would profit by examining what resides within their hearts. What griefs or sorrows, pains or pleasures, limits or freedoms, confusions or clarities, sadness or joy, and stagnations or circulations are held within the center of his being?

For the law of attraction operates whether or not man is consciously aware of it. Through the movement and the circulation of the light of man's awareness as he reflects upon his heart, he will begin to see and understand more clearly, the framework and the meaning of earthly life.

Then, with sincerity and humility, man may ask of the Divine to help align him so that love becomes the ethic and harmony becomes the state in which man lives and moves and has his being.

The law of harmony can be satisfied through intimate relationships with self or others in the earth. The fulfillment of this law, however, comes from the individual's desire to continue to seek the love of the Divine by allowing the desires of his soul to overcome the earthly desires of his body and mind.

### The Law of Desire

**"Not my will, but your will, Father,
be done in me and through me each day"**

The fifth center or the throat chakra is the place wherein resides the law of desire, soul-will, or spiritual determination. Through the operation of this law, all forms of manifestation are possible.

There are many desires that man experiences in his earthly tenure, for desire can be of the physical, mental, emotional, or spiritual natures of man.

In the body of man, these desires arise from his physical or biological needs. There is the desire for sustenance, for quenching of his thirsts, for warmth and shelter, and for the gratification of his sexual compulsions.

In the mind and emotions of man, there is the desire for companionship and the sharing of life in dialogue, conversation, and verbal intercourse. There is the desire for emotional well-being and health of the body and of the mind. There is the desire for wealth, and power, and position that so often accompany the awakening of the center for earthly power or the karmic body mind in man. Then there is the desire for love, to give and receive it while on the earth.

In the soul of man, there is the desire for illumination, growth, and fulfillment in and through the Divine.

Desire is the means through which the universe was created and maintained and sustained in its evolutionary movement.

Desire is the principle motivation within and without all manifestation. It was the desire of the Divine that began the song of creation. It was His desire for companionship that brought soul-specks into being. It was His desire for creativity that brought the experimental and experiential planet of love that is the earth, into being. And it was His desire for growth and life to be experienced in new ways that brought the soul of mankind into being.

Without the force of desire, there can be no creation, expansion, or movement. For thought and spirit - the pattern and the energy - in and of themselves, can do little. But through desire, the spirit of life can move through the pattern of mind and creatively manifest into the earth.

The law of desire can be seen operating on every level of the earthly-framework. Man, through the alignment of his four lower centers, can manifest and accomplish great works through the working of this law.

In much of man's earthly life, however, man dances with his own shadows and illusions and is blinded in his self-determinations. Those choices made in darkness and in ignorance, feed the wheel-of-life and serve to bind him ever more firmly to the things of the earth. The way of escape is for man to seek the light of truth and illuminate his darkness and to desire, above all else, the love of the Divine.

It is not, then, what the body or mind of man desires, but what the soul of man desires for his body and for his mind. For if one cannot pass through the barrier of earthly desires in this time of transition, then that one will lose himself and prevent himself from claiming the knowledge and wisdom of his true self.

It is never too late. In this day and in this moment, each may turn and face his God. Each may begin, as best as he understands, to live in accord with the Divine.

For the first will be last and the last will be first. And for each soul who begins the walk towards the Divine, there will be great rejoicing and celebration across the length and breadth of the heavenly firmament.

The law of desire can be satisfied in the earth through the manifestations and the gratifications of the things of the earth. The fulfillment of this law, however, is the releasing of all earthly desires and the taking up of one desire:

**To do the will of the soul, and thereby,**
**the will of the Divine, above all else.**

Through this determination, there will be a movement of man's awareness to the light, illumination, and the knowledge that can only be found in the truth.

## The Law of Truth

### "For TRUTH is in the 'I' of the beholder"

The sixth center, or spiritual eye, is the bearer of the law of truth. Although "truth" may exist in man's earthly experiences, each experience and incarnation and manifestation can yield only a portion of the one truth.

The law of truth allows man the freedom to escape his earthly limitations and to move wherever his curiousity and desire for knowledge and understanding may lead him. This access to truth will give man the gift of freedom from his enslavement to earthly thoughts and beliefs.

The law of truth acts in the body of man to awaken and cleanse and prepare the body for the eventual descent of his spritual awareness and illumination. The truth is the light of the Divine as understood and as it is existent in the moment. When bearing witness and acting in alignment with the truth, the power of the Divine that can be accessed through the crown chakra, begins to move and to flow.

Those who have gained access to the sixth vibrational awareness are those who have been pure in heart and in purpose; those who have struggled and surrendered to their own souls; those who have sacrificed the fulfillment of their earthly desires and temporal satisfactions for the lasting and ever fulfilling truth of relationship with the Divine.

If only man could taste the love, the joy and the rapture of the spiritual realms wherein there is intimate relationship with all souls and the Divine. It is beyond human understanding and experience, beyond any earthly gifts and experiences.

And yet, in this time, there will be the experience of this joy and this rapture within and on the earth. It is, and will be, within reach and sight of all those who have so little belief and so much misplaced faith, that heaven must descend and knock on their doors rather than they knocking on heaven's.

Then, the spirit of truth will set the soul of man free from the tyranny of those forces that would seek to control and undermine.

The satisfying of this law is man's access to truth and knowledge and visions and manifestations within his carnal shell.

The fulfillment of this law, however, is in the desire to be one with the Creator and the maker of all things. This desire for wholeness will lead man upwards to the realms of the seventh vibrational awareness or the law of love.

### The Law of Love in Oneness

**"Love the Lord your God with all your
heart, mind, and spirit and your
neighbor as yourself"**

The seventh center, crown chakra, or the cosmic consciousness center, is the bearer of the law of love Divine.

Love is the spirit that binds all things together. All thoughts, feelings, purposes, and manifestations become as one in the sight and in the presence of love Divine. Love is like a spiraling wheel that, through its turnings and revolutions, seeks to catch souls in the rhythm, rapture, and expressions that are love in motion.

From love there issues forth joy, peace, faith, hope, grace, mercy, and all the fruits and manifestations of the spirit. Through love all may be known and all may be experienced.

Whereas in truth there needed to be movement, in love one becomes the center of "All That Is" and all is ever-present in the moment.

This law governs all those who desire to be one with the Divine. It seeks to prepare the body by quickening and increasing its capacity to accept the gifts of wisdom, truth, and power from the Almighty. Here the soul rightfully recalls its heritage and relationship to the Divine, and through this law becomes the means through which the Divine may manifest directly into the earth.

For in love, the Divine and the man that co-exist within the soul, can be made as one.

That God made man, that man made God, that enlightened one, then becomes a channel of blessing for the earth and for others, by not only practicing, but by being the active presence of the Divine.

All, then, is done in grace. All is done with compassion. All is done in understanding and with purpose that is of and through the Divine.

All is then in union and oneness through the law of love.

## IMAGE: INVOLUTION of LOVE IN ONENESS

### INVOLUTION of SPIRIT

| DIVINE LAW | LOVE IN ONENESS | LOVE OF TRUTH | LOVE AS DESIRE | LOVE IN HARMONY | LOVE IN MEMORY | LOVE THRU CREATIVITY | LOVE IN LIFE |
|---|---|---|---|---|---|---|---|
| LOVE | Love In Union | | | | | | |
| TRUTH | Light Of Love | Light Of Truth | | | | | |
| DESIRE | Love In Desire | Truth Of Desire | Will Thru Desire | | | | |
| HARMONY | Love In Harmony | Truth In Harmony | Desire In Harmony | Peace Of Harmony | | | |
| CAUSE and EFFECT | Love As Memory | Truth In Memory | Desire Of Memory | Harmony In Memory | Grace Of Memory | | |
| CREATIVITY | Love In Creativity | Truth In Creativity | Desire For Creativity | Harmony As Creativity | Memory For Creativity | Growth Thru Creativity | |
| LIFE | Love In Life | Truth In Life | Desire For Life | Harmony In Life | Memory Of Life | Creativity Thru Life | Spirit In Life |

## UNIVERSAL PRINCIPLES

The principles that follow are those that can form the foundations of man's life in the earth. These principles are simple in their form, but difficult in their application, for they embody the very core of the "seed" that is carried within the aspect of the law that they reflect.

*Live life in co-creative abundance*

*As one learns, so do we all learn.*

*There are no levels nor any distinctions within the heart of the Divine, for all are one.*

*The ear of the Almighty waits in loving expectation for the whispers of the prayers of his children.*

*Give a little, receive a little. Give much and you will receive much.*

*Do to others what you would have them do to you.*

*Seek the truth in all things, and it will set you free from all things.*

*Knock and the door will be opened, seek and you will find, ask and you will receive. But almost never in the way that you expect and always in the way you need.*

*Study to show yourself approved in the eyes of your Maker and act in accord with that approval.*

*Expect nothing and you will receive nothing. Expect much of the Divine and you will receive much in accord with the cup that you have fashioned and prepared to receive it.*

*Wheresoever one places his attention, there will his heart be also. So be wary upon what you focus. Stay awake and guard and protect the heart, for it is the gateway to the Divine.*

*Live your life in love. Love the life you live. For any other way is robbing yourself of the presence of the Divine.*

*Persevere. Be determined and courageous in your pursuit of truth. For what is counted in the heavens are not the results, but the attempt and the effort one has made to accomplish the purposes that he holds in his heart. Try, try, and try again.*

## HEAR O ISRAEL,

We call all those who are known as the ISRAELITES.
We speak not of those who are as the Hebrews,
But call forth those who are the Children of the
Light.

We call all souls who through this time and to
The time of 2012, are struggling and striving to
know and understand GOD within MAN.

We call all souls who seek the Divine in this time,
Whether from the sixth or the seventh,
Children of the earth or children of the heavens.

We call all souls who have brought GOD into their
awareness and have made Him an aspect and a
greater portion of their earthly lives.

These souls are known as O ISRAEL, the Awakened Ones,
The Aryans and the Enlightened Ones,
The Children of the Light and the Promised Ones.

We call all souls who seek the Light,
For they will all be blended,
To aid in transforming the earth.

We call all souls who have prepared and have chosen,
For they will enlighten and aid and strive always
To serve their earthly brethren.

We call all souls who desire to quicken mankind,
For they will move the earth's awareness,

From the THIRD to the FOURTH dimension.

*The ORACLES of LIGHT*

## 4.2 The NEW TEACHING

In each age of man, and in each cycle of learning within that age, there arises a need for the soul of man to grow into a new understanding and seek for a new way to apply a different facet or aspect of the truth.

For just as the needs of a child change as he moves through childhood, adolescence, young adulthood, and earthly maturity, so do the children of the Divine require different opportunities, understandings, and challenges as they move through their cycles of learning and grow towards spiritual maturity and awareness.

The truth, then, has always been the same, but what has changed through time and through the ages of evolution and devolution has been man's understanding of his relationship to the truth.

The Divine intent within these times of ever increasing change is to move the understanding of the truth in the mind of man into closer alignment and harmony with the truth which ever resides within the mind of the Divine.

From the perspective of ideas, concepts, and ideals, the "New Teaching" is not new, for these concepts have been contemplated, reflected on, and spoken about for millennia. But what is "new" is that, as this alignment continues, there will be an ever growing desire to seek for new and creative ways to apply the truth of this teaching in each individual's life.

The "New Teaching", then, is a call for all souls to a "new" application of that one truth in the earth.

The four cycles, phases, or stages of learning that mankind has moved through and experienced in this second ascendant age are also reflected in the experiences of each group of souls and each individual soul that walks the path of spiritual growth and awareness.

## THE FOUR PHASES OF MAN'S SPIRITUAL EVOLVEMENT

Each soul in the earth can be likened to a "candle" whose "wick" is the spirit of life and whose "wax" is that soul's manifested experiences.

Each soul, through desire and determination, chooses its earthly experiences, challenges, and opportunities and adds the "wax" of earthly existence onto the "wick" that is its life. These experiences vary in color, flavor, scent, and texture and are the uniqueness and the specialness that gives each soul its individuality. The "wax" of man's earthly experiences may be pure and pristine or they may be filled with sediments, entrainment, and impurities that cause difficulties in sustaining and maintaining the light of truth.

The shape of each soul candle and the nature of each experience that is added to the "wick" of life is determined by each individual's beliefs about his experiences and his choices acting through universal and Divine law.

Each soul candle is unique and special, and yet each is in relationship and each is the same in that the "wick" or the spark of life is a chord that connects each and every soul to the First Cause.

Each soul candle is then individual, and yet, at the very core of its being, one with all that is.

Near the beginning of this second ascendant age of man, when viewed from the heavens, was the cycle of darkness

# IMAGE: THE FOUR PHASES OR CYCLES OF SPIRITUAL EVOLVEMENT

| CYCLE OF TRUTH | NEW TEACHING | Phase Four: | SELF-RESPONSIBILITY |
| CYCLE OF MIND | CHRISTIAN AGE | Phase Three: | QUESTIONING |
| CYCLE OF EARTHLY POWER | MOSAIC AGE | Phase Two: | CONSCIOUS ACCEPTANCE |
| CYCLE OF DARKNESS | BONDAGE OR ENSLAVEMENT | Phase One: | BLIND ACCEPTANCE |
| "SOUL of MANKIND" | "SOUL GROUP" | "INDIVIDUAL SOUL" | |

THE FOUR CYCLES OF LEARNING OR EVOLVEMENT FOR MANKIND ARE ALSO REFLECTED IN GROUPINGS OF SOULS WITHIN MANKIND AND FOR EACH INDIVIDUAL WITHIN THE EARTHLY-FRAMEWORK.

or ignorance wherein mankind's conscious awareness was dimmed. If one were to fly over the earth in the midst of this cycle when the night sky was clear, one could see pin-points of individual lights from these soul-candles, and even groupings or whole communities that were illuminated, but the framework in which these lights of awareness existed was a framework of darkness.

As man's awareness evolved and moved through the cycles of earthly power and the awakening of his higher mind, more and more "wax" of earthly experience was added to the "wick" of his life.

Each cycle of man's learning was a continuum of gradually increasing light on the earth, with no clear demarcation where one cycle clearly stopped and another clearly began, for one flowed into the other and all was in transition. Within these cycles, these soul candles were patiently readied and prepared, layer upon layer, line upon line, waiting in expectation for the the earthly light of their lives to be replaced by the "fire" that exists as the spirit of truth.

In the fourth and final cycle of truth, the opportunity to be inflamed by the spirit of truth was given by the Divine.

This spirit descended and bore witness and worked through each soul candle that allowed itself to be instruments of the Divine. In the past 3000 years, there have been many who can be called great teachers, prophets, mystics, healers, and sages. Each in their associations and in the embodiment of their teachings of the truth, sought to enlighten others so that the earthly-framework could be moved from one of darkness to one of widely scattered light.

Each "Enlightened One" who illuminated others in the name of the Divine, met individual soul-candles with whom they were in conscious awareness. The earthbound souls who were blinded by the darkness of ignorance were given the light of knowledge. Those souls who were enslaved and limited by their beliefs, were shaken, battered, and pummeled by the power in the thoughts and words of truth until their barrier-like beliefs either crumbled or they turned away in self-protection. Those who questioned and were skeptical, were moved by direct and personal experience of the truth. And those who had searched, sought, and desired with their hearts, minds, and souls the truth, were illuminated by the power of the most Holy Spirit of the Divine.

Whether in the eastern thought or the western thought, all who taught and were an embodiment and a living example of their teaching, exposed to man's awareness an aspect and a facet of the one truth.

In this time of transition, all soul candles are being softened by the crucible of physical, mental, emotional, and spiritual earthly experiences. Their shapes and textures are being reworked, remolded, reshaped, and refashioned in accordance with their desires and their beliefs. The "wax" of earthly experience is being poured onto the "wicks" of their earthly lives. And the weight of their incarnational impurities that have accumulated throughout all their cycles of learning, are being drawn from them and released to the core of the Divine in the earth or taken upwards and released to the core of the Divine in the heavens.

And in a very real way, the "candle" that is man's soul has been lit from both ends.

## The Spiritual Evolvement of Groups within Mankind

In mankind's cycle of darkness, the mind of man was enslaved to his bodily needs and desires and moved towards a greater relationship with the earth, himself, and others over the course of time. In the cycle of earthly power, man evolved into greater acceptance and awareness of his bodily needs and desires and, through the increasing power of his emotional nature, found new and more creative ways to satisfy them. In man's cycle of mind, coupled with higher desires and emotions, there was a curiousity and a questioning about historical traditions and values and beliefs and new methods of exploration were devised. In the cycle of truth, there arose a greater desire to search for the truth in every facet and aspect of man's existence.

The four cycles or phases of spiritual evolvement for mankind of blind acceptance, conscious acceptance, questioning, and personal responsibility for the search for truth, are also reflected within specific groupings and gathering of souls within the body and the history of mankind.

One such grouping of souls were called Israel and are but one example of many of the groupings of the children of the light as they manifested in different times and different regions of the earth.

In that particular time nearly 3000 years ago, the children of Israel were in a state of blind and conscious acceptance of their enslavement in the lands of Egyptian knowledge. They were slaves, not only physically, but had allowed themselves to be mentally caught in the mundane mediocrity of earthly existence. They lived in the midst of their Egyptian masters' beliefs in many gods and their trust and belief and hope in the one God had faded due to the pain and hardship of their captivity.

Then that one known as the lawgiver or Moses came to them and, through the use of the power and the wonder inherent in bearing witness with the truth, overcame the forces of earthly-power (as embodied by the Egyptians), broke the chains of bondage, and lead these people into the desert. There they wandered for forty years until their questioning and their skepticism about the nature of their God were answered either through transition or transformation.

They were then ready to be led into the "Promised" lands and to allow all the promises or covenants of the Divine - with those who would be His people - to be fulfilled.

At that time in their awareness and evolvement, the Divine - through Moses - gave ten principles, laws, or commandments by which His people should abide.

But because the heart of those children were hardened, they could not easily understand how these ten principles should be lived in the earth. In an effort to aid the people in their understanding, those in authority took these ten principles and fragmented them into hundreds and hundreds of rules, regulations, and doctrine.

After a time, rather than clarifying, the rules and regulations began to confuse. Rather than lighting the path to the Divine, they obscured it. Rather than continuing to grow in relationship to the truth, these children became more and more bound, imprisoned, and enslaved by their own limiting beliefs.

Thus, the same methods that served to move individuals through one phase of spiritual evolvement were the same methods that imprisoned and prevented them from moving into the next.

And there arose a need for a new understanding and a new application of the one truth in the earth.

The soul that was known as Jesus the Christ or the Annointed One, was then sent by the Divine to those children who had prepared the way for his earthly descent. He taught, demonstrated, and embodied a new understanding of the truth. He taught that the soul of man was not made to live its earthly life by rules and regulations, but should rather live in accordance with Divine law which is as the very words which emanate from the mouth of God.

This great Soul who was a child of the light and a son of God as well as the son of man, taught and lived the principle of love.

For the very essence and the core of all the great teachings of the one truth is the triangle of love which calls for individuals to love God, themselves, and others with equality, with acceptance, and without exception.

Through this great soul's life, death, and resurrection, the veil of forgetfulness was removed from the collective unconscious of mankind and a clear way to intimate and personal relationship with the Divine was provided.

Jesus and Mary took on the law of cause and effect, which was the wheel-of-life that mankind spun upon, and overcame it. This master soul who, as Adam and Eve had led the way into physicality and, as Jesus and Mary, fulfilled the law and showed mankind the way to escape into Divine consciousness.

For there are many paths, but there is only one way.

That way is for each soul to move into the love and illumination within the mind of the Divine.

Through his resurrection he demonstrated that the spirit of life could overcome earthly death and that man could be transformed, accelerated, and quickened. Each of Jesus's seven centers or chakras was aligned and attuned to the Divine such that the first chakra vibrated as rapidly as the seventh and, in this way, he could ascend - body, mind, and soul - into the heavens.

That one known as Buddha experienced this same quickening of his chakras into attunement with the vibrations of the seventh center following the days of silence beneath the tree that gave him new life. Buddha's desire was to receive the heavenly food of the Divine and was no longer content to live solely on the fruits of the earth.

That one known as Babaji of the Himalayas, who lives near the library of the earth, is another that has experienced this all encompassing quickening. And there have been many other soul-candles that have been inflamed and quickened in this same manner.

Following the life of that one known as Jesus, the lack of understanding of the people of how to live love in the earth and the desire of the few to control the many, the teaching was once again fragmented and the spirit and the meaning of love became obscured by the myriad of rules, regulations, and limitations of formalized philosophy.

And the light of truth was once again blended with the darkness of man's ignorance, and there was confusion and distortion.

This same pattern can be seen in all earthly philosophies in all times and cultures and regions in the earth. All are children of the Divine and those who seek the spirit of truth are given many opportunities by the Divine to experience it.

Just as the Mosaic Age strove to break the bonds and enslavement of ignorance, and the Christian Age served to break the barriers of karmic belief, the "New Teaching" has come to unify the duality of man's awareness and seeks to find a "new" way to apply oneness in the earth.

## The Spiritual Evolvement of the Individual

These same four cycles or phases of learning that apply to the group of souls within the body of mankind, are also reflected in the evolvement of the individual.

### Phase One: Darkness - Unaware Acceptance

As a child in the earth, the individual is often exposed to the religious or formalized approach to spirituality. In this phase, there is little thought and a deep sense of blind acceptance of what is shown to be acceptable behaviour regarding all facets of the religious life and framework.

Songs are sung, books and scriptures are read, and prayers are learned and recited by rote. This phase is characterized by a non-questioning attitude and a sense that things are the way they are because they simply are that way.

### Phase Two: Earthly Power - Conscious Acceptance

The second phase of "conscious acceptance" usually occurs as a youth - but can extend into early adulthood - and is the phase that entraps most souls within the earthly-framework.

What occurs to the individual is full and conscious acceptance of the rules, regulations, boundaries, dogma's, values, and structures of that formalized or institutionalized religious-framework. These guidelines allow the individual to remain a basic non-thinking person, allowing others, within that framework, to do their thinking for them.

Individuals within this second group are instructed on how God should be found and how He should not be found.

The paths that are acceptable will be clearly marked and the paths that are unacceptable will be condemned, judged, and disallowed.

These individuals most often become "missionaries" and feel a need to educate the world about the right and correct way to God and often seek to demonstrate the incorrectness and wrongness of the spiritual paths that others walk. These individuals are fundamental and basic in their thinking and feel comfort in knowing they have all the answers to earthly and heavenly existence.

### Phase Three: Mental Development - Questioning

The third phase of spiritual evolvement, or "questioning", can occur as early as adolescence and as late as full adulthood and is characterized and initiated by a rejection of formalized or institutionalized forms of beliefs, philosophies, or religions.

This group includes those who are atheistic and agnostic in thought and those who are profoundly skeptical about God and spirituality. This group includes scientists, technologists, and other rational and objective seekers of the truth. Individuals within this group try to reason, ponder, and question the nature of truth from a variety of different perspectives and viewpoints.

This grouping of souls is loved in the heavens and much is shared with them in an effort to aid them to unravel the puzzle that is earthly existence or life. There is an effort by those in the heavens to expose them to the wonders and the workings of the Divine.

There is a desire in the etheric to show these individuals that God is deeply personal. That He will talk with you, experience your life with you, respond and fulfill all your needs and desires, and will love you without conditions.

## Phase Four: Seeking the Truth - Personal Responsibility

This heavenly or Divine phase of growth in spiritual evolvement is a unique and self-determined and self-designed way of learning and development.

This fourth phase involves the acceptance of personal responsibility and involves self-study, research, and applications of ways that will awaken the soul or the spirit of man within. It is the search for truth through a willingness to entertain new ideas, seeking better ways and methods, and crystalizing those ideas through personal experiences.

There follows the growth of the desire within the individual to rely, depend, and trust in the Divine to provide knowledge and assistance and the understanding that the spirit is life and it is also love.

There is a desire for partnership or union with the Divine, so that each can act for and through the other in a way that would allow co-creativity to express. The individual feels a sense of surrender and acceptance and a willingness to be a child of God and a child of the light. And there is faith that the Father will light the way, reveal the path, and provide all the answers needed.

Once the individual moves his conscious awareness to the Divine, then he allows an experience of the Divine. Once he has an experience of the Divine, than that individual is willing to work in the name of the Divine and live in the light of God, and recognize the fruits and the works of God as the great one manifests in the earth.

As the consciousness of the earth evolves, there will be a greater and greater movement of individuals into this fourth phase of awareness and spiritual evolvement.

Many individuals will also choose to remain in the first, second, and third phases in this time of earthly transition.

But it will be those individuals who move to claim personal responsiblity for themselves and their alignment and attunement with the Divine who will help to awaken the mind and soul of mankind and move the earthly-framework from the third to the fourth dimension.

## THE RISE IN INDIVIDUALISM

The fourth phase of man's spiritual evolvement is the phase that gives birth and supports the growth of individualism.

Within this movement, there is an understanding that each individual is special and unique and beloved by the Divine. That each soul will be pursued by the Divine in ways that are unique and specific so that communion and awareness can occur at whatever level is needed, at whatever level is required, at whatever level allowed is by that individual.

The Divine can be seen as a wonderful lover that is in constant and unending pursuit of those He loves. And for each soul, He desires only their return into an awareness of His presence, their return to full knowledge of Himself and themselves, their return to an expression of all their creative abilities, and for the two lovers to become as one.

The Divine delights in the variety, spontaneity, and imagination of man's creative expression and, as man expresses creatively, the spirit of the Divine will bear witness within man's earthly and heavenly expressions.

There are no set rules or regulations on the path to the Divine. There is only the taking on of responsibility for the self in its relationship to the Divine. There are no easy ways nor are there set prescriptions or recipes of what can and cannot be done.

The result, in these times of transition, will be the dissolution of the institutions and rigid structures of philosophy and religion. Many who are caught in the first and second phases of spiritual evolvement will experience tremendous pain and grief over the dissolution of their beliefs.

In this time, the growth of the soul and the expansion of the individual will be through intimate experience and relationship with the Divine.

## GLOBAL ONENESS IN AND THROUGH LOVE

The foundations of the new harmony is a global awareness of oneness through the principle and the vibration of love.

Love is the principle that moves man's consciousness from one dimension to another. It is the ethic and the basis for the experiment and the experience within the earthly-framework. It is the motivator and the instiller of faith through the active presence of the Divine. And all who seek will be blended in and through the vibration of love.

Oneness is a reflection of the truth and the outcome of mankind's present cycle of growth. In this time, oneness will no longer be an ideal or a theory, but will be practically and pragmatically applied and integrated into every facet of man's life.

Politically there will be movements towards one world government. Economically, there will be movements towards one form of currency. Socially there will be movements towards one language, one race, and one global community. Philosophically, there will be a movement towards one spirit, one unified field, one time, one mind, one creator and one evolver of all the universes.

The rules, regulations, and spoken and unspoken customs that acted as barriers to oneness, will be dissolved. With this dissolution, there will be pain, anguish, and turmoil.

This pain of labour will continue until the earthly-framework and the heavenly-framework are in perfect alignment and attunement, as they were meant to be from the very beginning.

All that had seemed so wrong within the evolution of mankind will be righted within this time of transition. And the alignment of the earth with the heavens will be the fulfillment of God's Divine Plan for the soul of man.

## SEVEN PREPARATIONS, PRINCIPLES, & PROMISES OF THE NEW HARMONY

Even though the path that each individual walks on his journey back to the Divine is unique and is special, there are similar universal preparations, principles, and promises of the Divine that will form the very foundations of the emerging NEW HARMONY upon the earth.

The seven preparations are:

• _Heart-felt Belief_ - That through your knowledge and love in and through your image of God, you can become it.

• _Prayer, Meditation, Self-observance_ - Ask from your heart and the heavens will hear. Listen with your heart in the silence, and the heavens will respond. Look, and you will see the wonders of God's hand in your life.

• _Loving Service_ - Find ways to serve others that are in harmony and accord with your image of God.

• _Trust & Allow_ - Trust that the Divine is working in your life in often wondrous and surprising ways, and allow these ways to occur to you and through you.

• _Acceptance_ - Accept the gifts and the hardships. The knowledge and the ignorance, within yourself and those others with whom you associate.

• _Desire_ - Desire that the Divine be in your life, and He will be there. Expect the best from

Him, for you are his children and He is the father and the mother of all, and it will be provided.

- *Co-creative Expression* - Search for new ways to express your talents, abilities, and skills creatively in the earth.

The seven principles upon which the new harmony will be founded are:

*Oneness* in and through *Love*

*Peace* in and through *Harmony*

*Freedom* in and through *Truth*

*Fulfillment* through *Co-creative Manifestation*

*Acceptance* through *Self-responsibility*

*Transformation* through *Transition*

*Communion* through *Service* to others

The seven promises or covenants of the Divine with mankind that are given as gifts from the preparation and the manifesting of these principles are:

- If one simply believes in the Divine, the path and the *way* for each individual will be shown.

- If one *asks*, you will be heard and there will be a response from the heavens. If you knock, the door will be opened. If you seek, you will find.

- If you *give*, you will *receive*. As you move towards *love*, love will move towards you.

- If you place your *trust* and *faith* in the Divine, nothing is impossible.

- With the Divine, one may access unlimited knowledge, wisdom, and illumination.

- With the Divine, one may maintain an intimate and personal relationship with the *First Cause* and all those in all the universes and all the dimensions. In this way, you will be made *whole*.

- With the Divine, one may manifest the power and wisdom of the Divine in co-creative expression in the earth. To give in loving service to God, self, and others.

There are no boundaries nor limitations with the Divine. There is abundance and living and sharing in truth. All things are possible and all things that are the Father's will be yours if you will be His people and allow Him to be your God.

## 4.3 SIGNS, OMENS, EXPECTATIONS
### (1992 - 2000 AD and Beyond)

This time of transition is a time of unprecedented changes that will impact the body, mind, and soul of mankind. It is a time when all the seed-thoughts and actions that have been planted by man in the past are now bearing fruit.

In this day and in this way, each individual, group, mass, or class of mankind are having to meet themselves. Through this meeting of self, there will be the opportunity to clearly choose whether to follow the light or to follow the darkness.

There is no delight in the heavens over what has and must yet transpire on the earthly-framework. There is a deep sense of sorrow and grief that the past choices of mankind has led to this present time of testing, turmoil, and tribulation.

But in the heavens, there is also the wisdom that in order to salvage the soul of mankind and bring redemption and salvation into their hearts and minds, trauma and crisis may be the only way that some self-imposed barriers are penetrated and broken so that man can have the opportunity for intimacy with the Divine once again.

To that end, many spirit and light beings have responded to the call in the heavens and have come, at this time, to aid by giving light, love, and illumination to each earthbound soul who suffers and asks for help from the Divine.

In this Final Crusade between the forces of light and the forces of darkness, some souls will choose to clothe themselves in the armour that is of virtue and brandish the sword that is of truth. The souls who fight the battle for dominion within and without, and endure until the end, will be harvested through the fulfillment of all their covenants with the Divine, themselves, and mankind.

Those others who choose the darkness will be swept from the earth by the winds of change, to be nurtured and taught in the heavenly dimensions and given yet another opportunity, in the distant future of the earth, to cleanse and purge themselves once again.

For the Divine has willed that no soul shall perish, nor will it ever be lost or forgotten.

The purpose of sharing what will occur in this final decade of the millennium is to allow those who desire a part in the work of the Divine to help prepare the way in themselves and in others for the final descent of the spirit of truth onto the earthly-framework.

The servants and the handmaids of the Divine will labour to give birth to a new awareness on the earth and their labours will not be out of fear nor dread, but will be as a labour of love.

For remember that, in these times of great changes, it is not where one resides physically on the earth that is of importance. Nor is it in man's state of mind. But rather, it is where man's heart and awareness resides spiritually that will allow the evolution of man from the third to fourth dimensional awareness.

Fear not, then, and remember always that if you but ask of the Divine, it will be given. Listen and you will hear His reply. Look, and you will find His hand in yours to lead and guide you through the valleys of death and over earth's troubled waters.

## AN OVERVIEW OF THE FINAL DECADE
## OF THE MILLENNIUM

There is a fear on the face of the earth in this day. There is a sense that something is incorrect and not as right as it once was. There is an anxiety in mankind that is brought about by the ever quickening changes and the lack of seeming control, sense of boundaries, and stability.

There is a sense that, no matter how one struggles to hold and to maintain, the barriers of earth's social-frameworks are crumbling and in increasing disarray.

There is a growing instability in earth's political systems as world leaders face their own and their countries' deaths, reformulations, insurrections, and resurrections. Whether it is the kidnapping of those in positions of political power or whether it is the kidnapping of the political process itself by those who would seek to control, the break-down of man's trust in political systems will continue as the decade progresses.

There will be changes in the earth's climate and in the movements of the lands and in the flows of the waters and the rush of the earthly airs.

The changes in the world's climate will cause severe droughts in Africa, India, southern portions of North America, and in parts of Russia (Soviet Union). The droughts will negatively impact food production and there will be famine. And yet, even in the famine there can be heard the call to oneness, for there will be a tremendous need to share what food remains with others who face starvation around the world.

There will be a growth in understanding that the earth is a living organism and that no one individual, family, company, or country deserves nor has the right to control, manipulate, and maintain the balance of power with natural and agricultural resources.

There will then be a struggle between those who control and have, and those who need, but have not. One will strive to maintain and the other will strive to gain control of these resources. This struggle, when blended with diminished food production, mass starvation, and growing poverty will impact on the world's economy.

The world's and individual nation's economies will experience dramatic and rapid fluctuations that range from the very highest heights to the deepest depths. This movement will disorient and confuse the peoples of the earth such that they will not know what to do to meet their daily needs. Should one buy today and sell tomorrow, or sell today and buy tomorrow? Should one spend his money or save it? Should food be stored or should one continue to allow the stores to store food for them?

There will be a movement, as the decade progresses, towards a single type of currency. More and more economic alliances will be formed between nations and blocks of nations (as has occurred in Europe). And this movement will take on urgency with the dissolution of the island-continent of Japan.

Many individuals will be stretched to the point where they will experience breakdowns physically, mentally, emotionally, and spiritually. In turn, the breakdowns of families, communities, municipalities, and whole regions will tear at the very social fabric of the earth.

And each individual will, in a sense, be brought to their knees in an effort to re-awaken them to the Divine within and without.

## Earth Changes in this Final Decade

The sign or omen of the changes in the earth's climate will be the intensity and the changing patterns of the winds of the earth. In the wake of these winds, there will be the shiftings, rumblings, fracturings, and the breaking-up of the earth's lands.

The west coast of North America will experience gradually increasing and intense earth movements that will culminate in the great quake in that region. The flow of the waters from the St. Lawrence will be altered from the Atlantic Ocean to draining into the Gulf of Mexico. This alteration will result in an inner sea within that continent.

In South America, the flow of the Amazon will also be changed with the rising and the lifting of the mountainous areas in and around that continent.

Mexico, which is the place of joining between the North and South American continents, will experience many more rumblings and earthquakes that will be as though the ancient mexo-american knowledge must somehow be shaken into man's conscious awareness.

In the European regions, there will be tremendous winds that will harbour greater climatic changes. The United Kingdom, and especially England, will experience difficulties with the rising waters and extremes of climate. Portions of France will be submerged with some waters reaching as far inland as Paris.

In eastern Europe, the movements of the lands along the faults that pass through Hungary, Yugolslavia, and the Balkan states of Latvia, Estonia, and Lithuania will cause havoc and will cause Russia to experience difficulties with the flows of transportation, communication, and the earthly waters. The change in the flow of waters will negatively impact the great grain growing regions of the Russian nation.

In India, there will be tremendous rumblings and land movements in the very heart of that nation known as the library of the earth. India will experience a great loss of life, first due to drought and famine and then due to the increased rains, monsoons, and hurricanes to such a degree that it will seem that humanity is simply washed into the sea.

China will be awakened in this time and there will be an increasing movement towards spiritual awareness. For so long, the people's of China have been disallowed from their pursuit of the truth. This "sore" of spiritual denial that has seethed and bubbled beneath the skin, will seem to fester and burst upon the awareness of those peoples.

The eastern coast of China will be impacted by the tidal waves that wash ashore from the dissolution of Japan, with the waters reaching up to 250 miles inland. The southern portions of the Asian continent along the shores of Vietnam, Thailand, and Cambodia, due to the sheer force and dismay of humanity residing there, will experience climatic difficulties and tremendous winds.

The people's of Africa are in such difficulty and decay morally, physically, and spiritually that a great portion of this continent will be dismantled, not through earth changes, but through disease, drought, famine, and the shifting of the earth.

Australia will also be impacted by the shift and it will be as if portions of that great island-continent simply fall away into the seas or disappear into itself.

## The Rise of Light and Darkness

There will arise, in this final decade, a number of unusual people who have come to aid and be as voices in the wilderness. They will attempt to guide and lead the people of the earth from their sense of loss, confusion, and dismay into the light of Divine awareness and the peace of the new harmony.

Some of these earthly people will hear and respond to their message, but there will be many others who do not. As a result, many of these voices will be silenced through exile, imprisonment, or murder by those who, in their ignorance, would not or could not hear.

There will arise in this time, two witnesses of the light who are profound spiritual leaders. They will speak out in the cause of commonality, oneness, and manifested love in the earth. There will be revelations given to mankind and they will have about them, a sense of prophetic awareness.

And they will help prepare the way for the coming of the World Spiritual Leader who will show himself at the end of these troubled times.

There will be upon the earth the days of darkness that will be followed by a tremendous light and a sense of rapture in the skies.

Other planets of this solar system will be seen and re-discovered in this decade and, as they arise in man's conscious awareness, they will impact man's spiritual evolution. For one of these planets is the one the ancients called Aman. This planet will return from its long sojourn in the darkness of space and illuminate the earthly skies and aid in the cleansing spin that will prepare mankind for his and the earth's shift in conscious awareness.

Divine instruction will be given into the midst of humanity, for the angels will descend and walk and talk with men. In this time, mankind will be called in all ways, from the trauma and crisis of physicality to the experience of the heavens on the earth. For the promise of the Divine is that each individual will be met at the place he allows himself to be met by the First Cause.

Due to mankind's confusion and dismay, there will also arise two other "voices" that are charismatic, persuasive, and influential. They will rise, in this decade, to positions of earthly power and will claim that they are instruments of the Divine, whereas in reality, they will be the instruments of that one known as Lucifer.

Within man's understanding and within his records and memories, these two would be as the Anti-Christ and his prophet.

To many of the children of the light, these two will appear familiar and the children will intuitively know the true source of their earthly-power to be the darkness. This sense of familiarity will be due to having seen, known, and struggled with these two in the past during the first ascendant cycle of man.

In this final decade of the millennium, remember always to look for the highest good in all earthly circumstance and situations. Place your beliefs and your faith in a God that will personally share with you, give you knowledge, and will empower you from within.

Those who come in this time of transition and claim, profess, and demonstrate the tricks, illusions, and skills of a magician, should never be taken as the First Cause or a consequence of that same.

## EXPECTATIONS FROM 1992 TO 1997

The period from 1992 to 1997 is one of increasing change and stress to all levels of the earthly-framework. There is such an interplay between the forces that comprise the light and the darkness that will impact the socio-economic, political, and environmental systems that each year will be discussed separately and in detail.

### The Year 1992

**For the greater part of the year mankind will experience stabilization * Global drought and famine precipitates conflict between "have's" and "have-nots" * Global economic uncertainty with deep and rapid fluctuations in world stock markets in the Fall * Financial stress leads to continuing decay of social-frameworks ***

The year 1992 will for the most part, be a year of stabilization for mankind. For many it will be a year that will allow, both individually and collectively, to -in a sense - catch their breath. It will be a time of realignment and refocusing from the stressful growth period of 1987-1991. Although much will surface in mankind's awareness concerning global socio-economic, political, religious, and environmental difficulties, little movement will be manifested towards solution of these deep seated issues.

During 1992, there will be a deep thread of economic uncertainty running throughout all aspects of the world. The world currencies will be found to be less and less useful as a means of standardized value and this will result in a growing movement by people and their political leaders to seek some form of meaningful change. The quandry, however, will be the nature and the method of implementing this much needed change and, as a consequence, nothing of substance will be accomplished and the uncertainty will carry-over into 1993.

There will be an increase in global political "rumblings" brought on by the drought, diminished world food supplies, and famine in various regions of the world. Those countries who have excess food supplies will have a strong desire to hoard, while other countries face mass starvation. This inadequate and inequitable food supply in and around the globe will grow into a major political issue as 1992 progresses.

India, China, Phillipines, and Russia will also experience difficulties regarding their political systems and their leadership in this year.

The world's social-frameworks will continue to suffer decay due to the presence of financial stress and worry of the family and community units. The financial stress is due to the continuing confusion and dismay around gold and currency standards. There will result, particularly in the western hemisphere, a greater and greater rate of family breakdown and dissolution. Some family units, in the face of this financial crisis, will seek to pull together in an attempt to maintain their economic level and status. However, in general, the dividing will far outweigh the joining, and this will impact their communities and tear at the very social fabric of the earth.

Spiritually, there will be a type of calling to many people around the world. The issues at a basic survivalist level will cause many to re-examine their spiritual values and beliefs. These then will begin to re-establish their foundations and seek stability in existing religious and belief structures in an effort to fill the void of trust that was broken in the continuing instability of the world's economic and political systems.

### The Year 1993

**Global economic turmoil and dismay deepens * Scarcity of market produce and natural goods * Factory workers experiencing grave difficulty * Growing concern for third world countries due to drought and famine * The beginnings of the rise of the lost continent of Atlantis * Earth's climate begins to noticeably change in late 1993 ***

In the fall of 1992, the world's major stock exchanges will have experienced major dips accompanied by soaring interest rates followed by rapidly declining interest rates. These rapid fluctuations of key economic indicators will lead to a tremendous confusion over the true state of the world's economy and will result in a continuing and growing economic dismay throughout 1993.

There will be a growing sense throughout this year that time is, in a sense, on the move. For the shift in August of 1992 will begin to be felt and manifest in the earth such that 20 years of previous earthly events and experience will be compressed into a single year.

There will be more turbulence, movement, and difficulties with the waters in every portion of the earth, but especially evident in the Atlantic Ocean. It will seem as though there is a movement beneath the ocean waters, a murkiness, and a storminess, the cause of which is not identifiable, recognizable, nor explainable by scientists who are called to investigate this phenomenon.

The cause of this movement is the rise of the lost continent of Atlantis.

Many "new age" prophets and seers have predicted the rise of this lost continent within this time of transition, and 1993 will see the beginning of the fulfillment of those prophecies. There is a need for Atlantis and all that it symbolizes, to rise in the conscious awareness of mankind. The proliferation of books and articles concerning Atlantis at this time (1992) is a call to remembrance in the minds of men, whereas the rise of the lands in the Atlantic are the physical or tangible recollection of its former existence.

The movements of lands beneath the waters of the Atlantic will also affect areas within the waters of the Pacific. The result will be rumblings and moderate to medium earthquakes on the west coast of North America.

The movements of lands beneath the waters of the Atlantic will also create corresponding difficulties in the areas and regions around Greece. The physical connection between these two areas is a natural fault or strata that runs beneath the waters such that the rise of lands in the Atlantic impacts the lands around Greece. The karmic connection between these two areas is that Greece was a beloved colony of Atlantis and was greatly impacted with the demise and final destruction of the Atlantean continental civilization nearly 12,500 years ago. As this continent is resurrected in the minds and memories of men, Greece will be correspondingly impacted in this day.

In Russia in the year 1993, there will be an effort to reinstate communism. But by that year there would have been such an intrusion of capitalist thought into the economic and social structures of that nation, that this movement is seen as illogical, non-sensical, and irrational and will fail.

England will experience severe social and economic collapses and there will be grave concerns in the United States over the continuing economic deterioration and high domestic unemployment.

In South America, the peoples of that continent will experience more earthquakes.

In China, there will be the rise of a political leader who will become a significant voice and will move that nation towards more liberated thinking and activity than has previously been experienced.

There will be a growing movement by many people towards the churches and organized religious structures while at the same time, a deharmonizing or loss within the hearts and minds of long-standing members. This movement towards these organized belief structures is in response to growing earthly confusion and instability whereas the movement away is due to disenchantment and disillusionment with those same systems.

Although the Pope will make a great attempt in 1993 to reach out in service to mankind, there will be growing confusion in and around the Vatican.

The confusion in the Vatican surrounds "secret information" concerning that Church's involvement in politics, global economics, and the control and suppression of information that forms the very foundations of the Christian philosophy. This "secret information" would be found to reside in, and is linked with, the nations of Russia and Iraq. The issue surrounding this "information" would have surfaced in 1992 and will continue till 1995, and will cause great consternation and upheavals in the Catholic and other Christian churches.

The earth's climate will experience more and more difficulties which will be overt and noticeable by late 1993, for these climatic changes are but one component of this transitional drama that seeks to move man's motivation from the earth to the heavens.

## The Year 1994

**Financial stress on families-communities continues to worsen * Global media overtly unleashes astounding information - World Exposes Itself. * Global terrorism on the increase * Italy becomes "hot-bed" of covert global political, economic, and informational activities * Mass migrations of people due to food shortages and unemployment * Spiritual Masters preparing themselves for future earthly ministry * Climatic extremes and unusual weather affect the globe * Wildlife experiences migrational confusions and mass suicides ***

The global and economic trauma that continued through 1993 will flow into 1994. There will be less financial resources available to families and communities and there will be stress, strain, and confusion. But even in the midst of turmoil, neighbor will begin to help neighbor in physical, mental, and spiritual ways as this trauma seeks to reformulate each individual's ideas about the true meaning of earthly community.

The global media will move to educate mankind through, in a sense, the unleashing of information. This "information" which was held secret, purposefully distorted, or previously misrepresented, and is important for man's understanding, will be brought to the world's attention. This "information" will involve all facets of man's earthly existence from business, government, science, global economics, to man's religious institutions and spiritual beliefs. The media will release this "information" in a different way than it has in the past and it will be as if the world exposes itself in 1994.

Much of this information appears to have its source in southern Europe, in and around the area of Italy.

Italy will become a center of focus and a hot-bed of activity in 1994. There will be an increase in global terrorism that will be centered and greatly affect this nation. Italy will be a center for certain aspects of global economic and political activity involving Switzerland, Germany, North America, and even Japan as well as the source of "information" that leads to more global awareness and discernment.

There will be mass migrations of people all around the world which will be especially noted in the area of Europe. These waves of population movements from one area or region of Europe to another will be precipitated by the shortage of food, loss of employment, confusion, and the relaxing and dissolution of national or political boundaries that restricted movements prior to this time.

The peoples of India will experience an increasing sense of earthly groundedness as the drought persists and their mass starvations worsen in 1994.

In the northern parts of India, Nepal, and Tibet there are lost lakes, valleys, and special places that have been undiscovered by man to this time. Within these special places there reside Spiritual Masters who are preparing themselves for their emergence from the secrecy of their mystic lives and their entry into a public ministry to mankind. This emergence will occur when the circumstance and the times are felt to be appropriate.

The overt changes in the earth's climate that began to be apparent in late 1993, will continue into 1994 with changes and the flows and movements of earth's waters. These changes in water flows will greatly affect the earth's climate in certain areas. Regions that previously experienced a warm and temperate climate, would now be cold and snow-laden. Regions that previously experienced high levels of moisture or rainfall, would now experience drought. These types of variations will occur all over the globe.

The animals and wildlife, due to changes in climate and water flows, will experience anxiety, urgency, and confusion in their movements and migrations. Entire groupings of animals will be found to commit, in a sense, mass suicides due to the changes of winds, waters, and airs.

The compression of time and increasing flow of energy within and around the earth will impact each individual in a different way. Those who have prepared themselves for these times and allowed their quickening, will be energized and almost enthusiastic in their life and work. Those who have not prepared themselves will experience de-energization, extreme fatigue, and tremendous exhaustion in the year 1994.

## The Year 1995

**Apparent economic stability gives way in late 1995 to deepening global depression * Tremendous winds begin to encircle the globe * Outside heavenly bodies or planets found to be plotting an intercept course with the earth * Scientists baffled by the darkness in the skies * More nations clamour to join the European Economic Community in bid for survival * China experiencing spiritual and cultural rebirth * Alarming rate of rising water levels around the world attributed to rapid melt-down of the polar ice caps***

The year 1995 will be a year of apparent stabilization from the stress and strain of the previous two year cycle. People will once again be given the time to catch their collective breath. In the midst of this apparent political and economic stability, there will be a sense of spiritual and psychic anxiety, as if mankind is preparing itself for even greater change, turbulence, and turmoil, that is yet to come.

The year will usher in significant impacts to the earthly-framework.

The earth's climate will once again be altered with the advent of changes in the wind patterns that will be of such a nature and velocity that they will encircle the globe.

The impact from the heavens will be the movement of a constellation and the return and rediscovery of what scientists perceive to be an outside body to the solar system. This outside body, as it follows a path towards and around the sun, will gather in its wake fragments of rocks and debris from the asteroid belt that will increase the frequency and occurrence of shooting stars, meteors, and meteorites that impact the earth and other planets.

This will precipitate in man's conscious awareness, the possibilities of different types of climatic shifts and there will surface evidence of the shifting of the polarities of the earth.

And the light in the sky will be dimmed as if the earth will experience a prolonged and sustained eclipse.

There will be a sense of greater earthly economic stability for much of 1995 that will be false and unwarranted. Many will be drawn in by this false sense of security and will be trapped in the global markets when they become dismayed in the later portions of 1995 and into 1996.

There will be economic and political movements centered around Europe, for many nations and blocks of nations will desire to form stronger economic alliances with this region. There will be a sense of struggle and urgency in the global movement to combine different economies and nations into singular parcels or units, and as a result, there will be an economic intermeshing between North America and Europe to a greater extent than has been seen to this time.

China will experience a tremendous change in the desire by those peoples to return to spirituality and the seeking and experiencing of the power of love from within. This desire, as it manifests, will allow the individuals, groups, and the masses of China to grow as one and become a force against those others who seek to compromise the power within through the exercise of external power, manipulation, and control.

There will be more movements and activities in the Atlantic Ocean with corresponding activity in the Pacific Ocean. The activity in the Pacific, however, will generally go unnoticed and unheralded because it is not as closely monitored nor travelled as the Atlantic.

The "greenhouse" or warming effect will increase dramatically in 1995. This warming trend will increase the rate of melting of the polar regions, with a greater melting occurring in the north relative to the south pole.

The result will be an increase in the waters and fluids in the earth's oceans and changes in the fluid levels along coastal regions of the earth's continents.

This rate of warming and melting will alarm the scientific community for it is much greater than ever anticipated. The rising water levels will affect the geographic and topographic outlines of the earth and the waters and affect the faults and different associated strata.

### The Year 1996

**The "Voices in the Wilderness" are given more credence by the worldly wise * The North and Baltic seas are awash with difficulties * The fuse is lit on the 'wave of aggression' that washes over the Middle East * On the crest of this Middle Eastern Wave, a new leader rises to the top * India, Indonesia, and the Phillipines are inundated * Australian drought continues * Volcanic eruptions and earthquakes in Japan impact western Pacific Rim * The debate over the location of Atlantis continues * Winds uncover lost temple in African desert * Ancient 'City of Gold' discovered in the jungles of South America ***

There will be an obvious shift in the awareness of the media, politicians, economists, and worldly wise, giving more credence to the philosophies and messages that had been delivered by the voices in the wilderness to this time. There will, in general, be greater acceptance of these messengers by humanity as a whole.

The North and Baltic seas will experience difficulty in the movement of waters, transportation, and the migrations of marine life.

There is a rising concern in the Middle East in 1996 that could show itself as early as 1995 (dependent on the determinations made by the Muslim leadership). The Middle East will become a seething mass of unparalleled aggression. It will be as though those of the Muslim awareness are so imprisoned, encapsulated, and encased in their understanding of their "truth", that they will collectively desire to pronounce war against the world.

There is a Muslim political leader who will rise to prominence on this 'wave of aggression' and find a place firmly on the world stage. He resided in the outer ranks of those in power and will not receive notice until this time.

There will be more movements and turmoil in the regions around the Indian Ocean, Phillipines, and Indonesia with monsoons, tropical storms, and more and more water. The peoples of those regions will experience tremendous difficulties and it will economically devastate those regions.

Australia will continue to evolve into a dryer and dryer sand bar. Her people's will constrict themselves into the outer fringes and coastal regions of that continent and there will be less and less arable and useable lands. The unique wildlife of Australia will experience the same confusion as her peoples.

China along with the whole oriental block of lands that comprise the south eastern Asian continent, will be impacted by increasing volcanic and earthquake activities that are centered in and around Japan.

There are many factors that influence the timing of the dissolution and disappearance of earthly lands. In Japan, this dissolution will depend upon the determinations made by its leadership, the growth of technology and its application, the earthly memories in terms of geographic, geological, and climatological affects, and the karmic affects of the ancient Lemurian and Atlantean souls who are incarnate as Japanese in this time. All influence the eventual vanishing of these lands from the face and the memory of the earth.

There will be difficulties encountered in the area of the Great Harbour or Mediterranean. There will also be confusion in the memories of mankind over the location of Atlantis. Even though land is continuing to rise in the Atlantic waters, some will persist in believing that Atlantis existed south of Greece and Italy and north of the coast of Libya. This confusion arises in man's collective memories, due to two island harbour city-states that were beautiful colonies of Atlantis that existed in the Mediteranean waters and were south of Greece and Italy. These city-states sank with the final demise of Atlantis and are being confused with the great civilization and continent that lay beyond the pillars of Hercules.

The changing patterns and movements of the winds in 1996 will sift the sands and uncover, in the desert between Egypt and Abyssinia (Ethiopia today), lost temples, knowledges, and remembrance of ancient civilizations.

There will also be a movement of people from Ethiopia into Egypt which will be constricted by the prevailing Muslim doctrines.

In the heavy jungles of South America, there will be the discovery of a "City of Gold" that was constructed by an ancient Atlantean pyramidic civilization. This city is filled with golden statues and ritualistic and symbolic constructions that are extremely powerful. There will be an awareness by mankind that those artifacts should not be touched or moved from that area.

### The Year 1997

**Unprecedented number of cases of environmental illness experienced * Mental-Emotional-Physical breakdowns on the rise * Heavens move closer to the earth * The Sound of Silence is heard * Volcanic eruptions and earthquakes increase dramatically * Confused politicians seek heavenly counsel * Russia, China evolve into spirituality * Saving of earthly know-ledge and history continues in the Library of the Earth * Great Pyramid and Sphinx continue to be probed for secrets ***

The year 1997 is a year in which there are the winds of change, the sifting of the sands, and the shifting of mankind closer to a state of Divine awareness.

There is a desire by the peoples of the earth to maintain what they have, but because of the confusion and break-downs on all levels of their being, they will find difficulty in doing so.

Physically, people will experience difficulty with environmental illnesses in the forms of skin rashes, tumours, eye problems, ear infections and diseases, and respiratory ailments. There is an intuitive awareness by the medical community in 1992 of what awaits mankind in 1997 such that efforts will be made over the next five years to develop the means to alleviate many of these ensuing ailments.

There will be a sense in 1997 that the heavens are approaching the earth. There will be reports of miracles, visions, and heavenly visitations in many places and by many peoples on the earth.

There will then be the awareness of a growing light.

There will be a movement or a shift of the earth by a heavenly body that will pass so close to the earth that the earth will be affected and will begin to spin in a completely different way. It will be as though the earth is speeded up and the winds, as a result, will increase dramatically.

Then there will be SILENCE.

This state of earthly silence will seem as if the rhythm of God has stopped for a time (this will not be true, but it will seem that way). This rhythm that underlies all of creation will be noticed due to its absence from man's perception. There will be an understanding that this aum, this sound, this heartbeat of the Divine will not be heard for a time.

This sound of silence will be a sign or omen heralding greater changes in the earth.

There will then be the volcanic activity and earth movements off the south east coast of Florida, then into the west coast of the United States, then into the area of Japan, then into the Mediterranean, then into Indonesia, and so on encircling the globe in a ring of fiery change.

There will be a number of volcanic eruptions with one long dormant volcano in the northern parts of Russia - near the north pole - erupting in 1997. These volcanic eruptions will help to quicken the global warming trend and cause more changes to the levels and flows of earthly waters. One such area of change will be the waters of the St. Lawrence.

The world political leaders will be in confusion over how best to help, direct, and guide mankind. They will confer with one another and many will also seek to confer with those in the higher or heavenly realms.

Russia, by 1997, will have redefined itself in terms of spiritual awareness. China will be in the midst of redefining itself in terms of the true art of warriorship or the power that lies within its peoples. In India and within the library of the earth, efforts will continue to preserve the knowledge, understanding, and history of mankind in books, tablets, and scrolls that are being hidden in caves and dark places. In Egypt, a greater mystic awareness of the secrets and truths contained within and without the Great Pyramid and the Sphinx, will lead to ever greater technical experimentation and probing.

In this time of great turmoil and tribulation, those who ask for Divine assistance will be heard and aided. Prayer from the heart will be an important remembrance for mankind in these times.

And this generation will live to see the rapture wherein the heavens descend to meet the earth in such a manner and in such a way that the mind and body of man cannot ignore nor dismiss it. If man has eyes, he will be able to see it. If man has ears, he will be able to hear the singing of the heavenly host and the music of the spheres on the earth.

Let those who have eyes to see, let them see. And ears to hear, let them hear the signs, omens, and expectations that herald and call the children of the light into service for the Final Crusade.

## THE FINAL CRUSADE

The final two years of the decade and the final two years of the millennium represent the apex and the climax of the present cycle of learning and the second ascendant age of man. All the years form a continuum, from the final destruction of Atlantis to this final two year cycle.

The earthly and the heavenly stages have been set. The opportunity and the drama must be played. And each must choose the nature of their armour and the nature of their sword that they will wield in the final battle of the Final Crusade for the spirit and soul of mankind.

For those who remain in the earthly-framework, the time of transition will culminate in and around 2012. There will be a rebuilding and a refashioning of the earth. But there will be a difference, for it will be done with joy and with peace. It will be a wondrous time, for there will be a new harmony that will prepare the way for the Golden Age of Mankind.

*Within this Golden Age of Mankind,*
*Love will reign upon the earth for a thousand years.*

## THE GREAT INVOCATION

From the point of Light
   within the Mind of God
Let light stream forth into
   the minds of men.
Let Light descend on Earth.

From the point of Love
   within the Heart of God
Let love stream forth into
   the hearts of men.
May Christ return to Earth.

From the center where the
   Will of God is known
Let purpose guide the little
   wills of men —
The purpose which the Masters
   know and serve.

From the center which we
   call the race of men
Let the Plan of Love and
   Light work out.
And may it seal the door
   where evil dwells.

Let Light and Love and Power
   Restore the Plan on Earth

Lucis Trust
United Nations Plaza
New York, N.Y.

# "PERSONAL VALIDATIONS"

## C.1 STORIES on AWAKENINGS

### The Story of Shelly

In 1981, there was a woman who was expecting a child. In her sixth month, the movement of the child within her womb had ceased. Her fears and concerns were not heard by the attending physicians. In her ninth month, the child was delivered and, when the chord that connected the child to her body was severed, the child died in the delivery room.

She was overcome with grief and loss. Twice before she had miscarried and now she faced the death of her child as it emerged into the earth.

The physicians had not placed any credence in her experiences and her inner knowingness and had dismissed them as the product of a woman's fears.

Her church offered her an Image of God that was one of punishment for an unknown crime that she had committed. She desired to bear children, but this God would not allow her to have them. Why? In her grief and sorrow she needed to know. Why?

She searched and explored for an answer to her dilemma. She grew to increasingly trust her personal experiences and intuitions. She formed support groups, investigated wholistic medical thought, sought for a new "Image of God" and, three years later, delivered a healthy child into the world in the light of her new-found spirituality.

# The Story of Simon

One cold winter's evening in 1983, on an acreage in the country, a man was faced with an opportunity to kill his earthly father or to spare his life.

In this man's youth, his father was an abusive and vile drunkard who had beaten and terrorized his mother and brothers and sisters. The man strived to find meaning in the midst of his seemingly irrational existence and he formulated, with the aid of distance and time away from his original family, a new image of God.

This new image of himself and his God began to solidify and crystallize in the 70's and he strove to think and act in accord with it. This new image was one of purpose, and principle, and meaning, and guidance and a lawfulness that was Divine and not of man.

And when this man felt firm in his new life and beliefs, he reached out, extended his hand to his still wounded father and invited him to live his dreams on the land they had acquired. For three years they lived together, and the father's dream to recreate his own youth for the benefit of his son and his son's family turned into a nightmare for all.

The father repeated his patterns of pride, arrogance, blind determination, rage, and intoxication and inflicted these on his son and his son's family. And the son repeated his patterns of honoring earthly parents and was bound by the fear that by his actions the innocent would be punished.

Brick by brick, piece by piece, day by day, this father was the instrument that sought to destroy all that his son believed of value. This father had dismantled all that his son had worked so hard to become.

All his beliefs that had flowed from his new image of God were shattered and in pieces. All his actions to do what was right and in harmony were compromised. His family was in pain. There was no joy. There was no peace. His prayers fell on deaf ears and he could no longer sense the presence of what he felt was the Divine.

And in the darkness of that winters evening that man came face to face with his father and he came face to face with himself.

There was a stillness. There was a quiet. But in the midst of this silent darkness, there was this man's anger, bitterness, rage, and despair. The opportunity he faced was to rid the earth of the vile and evil father who stood in drunkeness and rage before him or to allow him to live.

What should he do?

"Kill him. Kill him now for you, your family, and the world will be a better place without this evil drunken bastard. Kill him," the voice screamed in his head, "Don't think, do it."

But he did think, and with every ounce of determination that still remained within him, he turned from his father and went into his own home.

And in that solitude, and in his aloneness, the man awoke to what he was capable of doing and had almost done. He could kill another human being and he had been willing to do so. He had convinced himself that the world would be a better place for him having done so. And now he was lost.

He wept in sorrow and sadness over the loss of himself and he cried to the heavens, "Please. Please show me the Way. I don't know who I am anymore. I don't know what I've become. Please, show me."

And then, while on his knees in anguish, he beheld a vision. An angelic being stood before him whose eyes were as blue as crystal waters. He gazed into those eyes and they moved something within him. It was love. A love like no other he had ever experienced. He felt forgiveness for all that he had become and had been capable of doing. He was washed clean by the living waters that moved in harmony with this being's eyes and in the wake of this movement, there was only love.

And this man knew that the angelic being who stood before him was an image of his own soul. It was his true self and what he could one day become in the earth.

The vision lifted him from the depths of his despair and gave him hope and an experience of love that he would search to experience and re-experience again and again in the earth.

And it was this vision that would lead him on a search for God and Self.

## The Story of Laura

In 1982 a young mother began meditating. She had been encouraged to meditate by her neighbor and as these sessions continued, she began to sense a change occurring within her.

She willed herself to concentrate while in this meditative state and to permit herself to experiment with it. She had been given no earthly instruction as to what she should and should not do in meditation, but somewhere within her inner remembrance, this state of meditation was familiar.

On a sunny winter's day, she had decided to experiment in her meditative session by simply turning the "sun" on in her head.

As she concentrated on this mind-sun, she sensed a growing peace and silence and there began to appear a form within the mind-sun that filled her head. She focused on this form and grew in realization that before her stood the image of Jesus.

His gentle and knowing blue eyes gazed at her and she was held motionless in awe as a feeling of Divine Love emanated like waves, to her and through her. She basked in this Light that continued to embrace and surround her.

In the midst of this vision, she came to realize that all her deepest and most guarded thoughts, deeds, and actions were known by Jesus. Nothing was secret. That in spite of all her seeming sins and inadequacies, she was totally loved. This love was complete and all-consuming, and yet, liberating. So much so, that she allowed it to enmesh and permeate the core of her being.

That vision changed all her concepts about her connection to the Divine and four months later, she began to channel.

And yet another child had been called and responded to the call of the light.

# C.2 STORIES ON CLEANSINGS

## The Story of Rose

On this day in 1992, Rose contemplated that her life had been in turmoil for over five years. At that time, her marriage had disintegrated. She had met and fallen in love with another man. Caught in the throes of this duality, she had separated from her spouse, had purchased her own home, and had grown independence. Her guilt, however, disallowed her from either terminating her marriage or joining her lover. While both parties waited for the outcome of her decision, Rose sought to understand this untenable situation. She was a true soul. How could this have happened to her?

Unable to gain peace and clarity, she turned to God. She had awakened to her learning and sought to purge herself from her fears, guilt, self-denial, and self-castigation. For five years she prayed, participated in therapy, and walked a tight-rope of her earthly and spiritual learning. Rose came to understand that this duality was a test of what she was willing and not willing to live. She could choose to live in truth by joining with her lover or she could return to her husband. No one could make this vital decision for her and Rose abdicated from inflicting pain on either man. Meanwhile, her own pain grew. It became comfortable. It allowed her to punish herself daily.

Five years after this drama began, Rose was a different person. She felt God in her life. She began to release her fears about the future. She had travelled this far and had survived. She experimented with allowing herself guilt-free days. Those days felt good. With growing clarity, she began to speak and move in truth. She realized that God simply wanted her to speak and move in truth. She began to love herself and to understand the pathway of her learning. As she loved herself more, she experienced more love for the Divine plan within her life. It was then that she could move in love, not only for herself, but for all concerned.

God and Rose walked the path in love and truth.

## The Story of Mary

On this day in 1991, Mary stood in the court room, facing the judge. She was awaiting the decisive outcome of her divorce trial and she listened to the judge's every word.

As she watched this stranger, she commented inwardly how much easier the English language had become. She had lived in this foreign country for over thirty years. She remembered the fear she felt when the boat had docked in New York and she heard the strange language which she was to adopt.

She glanced over at her husband. He was standing at alert. She knew his reaction to legal authority. It was her saving grace. He would acquiesce to the findings of the court. She breathed a sigh of relief. Now the abuse would stop.

Her mind reeled back 40 years and she visualized herself as a young woman. She had desperately wanted to become a nun. It had been her lifelong dream for even as a child she had been aware of God's presence as she survived the labour and death camps. When she met the young man who was to become her husband, she became confused and forgot her burning desire to serve within a convent order. That momentary forgetfulness cost her her dreams, dignity, and her self.

She wondered about her four children. They were adults now, with families and dreams of their own. They stood beside her, awaiting the judge's determination. She wondered at the nature of their strength for together they had journeyed a path to hell and back. She and her children had survived rampant emotional, mental, and physical abuse at the hands of her husband.

Mary's husband was an embittered and cruel man who had levied terror and control within their home for 40 years. In spite of repeated atempts by Mary to placate this man's pain and frustration, nothing had soothed the monster who dominated the family. Alcohol had served to fuel the passion of his destructive tendencies.

Mary stood quietly praying. She had never, in all the years of marriage, stopped praying. God had always been, and would always be, present in her life and her heart. She wondered why she had had to experience this oppressive marriage. She had always felt that it was her duty to maintain a semblance of family life. As the years had passed, she had struggled more greatly to understand God's plan for her life. In the midst of her constant pain, her only solace was God's presence.

Her mind was called back to the courtroom. The judge was saying something about a Decree Absolute and an injunction against her husband. Something seemed to inwardly sweep over Mary. It was relief, freedom, and a knowledge that the marriage was finished.

But there was something else. In that moment, Mary came to realize that God had simply wanted her to stand up and say "No.". For forty years, she had lived a life of victimization. She had forgotten that God always empowers the individual with the right of decision making. She had abdicated and suppressed her rights and her dreams. Mary was now ready to assume her own power. She was now ready to say "No.".

As the judge banged his gavel, Mary knew that God had granted her a divorce...not the court.

## The Story of Athena

On this day in 1992, Athena stood in the front hall of her Scottish home. Her husband had died unexpectedly four months earlier and Athena had been in a state of flux since his death. She knew that God was around her. She could feel his presence. It was as though a soft, warm light encircled her to give her strength and consolation. She allowed this light to sooth her tattered nerves and to calm her mind.

As she stood in the foyer, she heard the word, "kundalini". She knew that kundalini meant cleansing and soul movement. She did not understand why she was hearing this word so clearly, however. Her knees buckled and before she could reach for the nearby oak railing, she found herself on the floor in a kneeling position.

Again she heard the word, "kundalini" as though she was being alerted to a process within her. Before she could make any movement, she began to feel pressure within her stomach. Something was rising within her. It could not be suppressed. It was physical, but it was also eerily spiritual. Once again, she heard the word, "kundalini", and as the voice repeated itself, she began to regurgitate. She could not stop the expulsion from deep within her being. She was sick as never before. Within minutes, the "kundalini" had ended.

Athena had experienced a soul cleansing. It had manifested within her physical body. It left her tired, but spiritually cleansed. Her mind was very clear after this experience for she was ready to emotionally bury her dead husband and to begin God's work in earnest.

All her life she had known and had been called to awaken others to this time of transition. She was now ready to proceed with her work in healing others and leading them to the light.

# C.3 STORIES ON SPIRITUAL EMERGENCE

## The Story of George

In the year 1896, a young North Dakotan boy attended a Methodist revival meeting. He listened as an evangelist delivered his message of temperance and devotion to God. George (age 13) was already aware that he had a calling. His awakening to this calling had occurred on the American prairies as he and his farming father had worked in harmony with nature. Together, they had struggled with the land and weather to "eek" out a living for the large family of 16 children.

When George was 23, his father died unexpectedly. The burdens of the father passed to the son. With his astute and brilliant mind, he persevered to ensure the financial safety of his family's home and the continued education of his siblings.

There appeared, one day, a man dressed in a uniform. He told this poor and sticken family that he was a Salvation Army chaplain and that he had come to aid them through the long Dakotan winter. The quiet determination and sincere humility of this stranger prompted George to welcome him into their humble home, and the chaplain stayed the winter.

George watched the 'spirit of patience' within this man that was present in his words and in his deeds, and determined to enter theology. George felt the calling to serve in some way as God's instrument and he felt theology was that way.

It was a number of years later that George graduated with his Bachelor of Arts and then enrolled in his year of Methodist mission. As he climbed into the pulpit to deliver his first sermon, he found that his voice was too husky to be heard and he was surprised that his childhood illness of diptheria could still be affecting his voice. He persevered and tried, every Sunday, to deliver God's word to his parishioners. But every Sunday he re-experienced the huskiness of his voice.

The odd thing about this was that in day-to-day situations, his voice was fine. Only on Sunday at the time when he needed to speak a sermon did the huskiness obscure his voice. George pondered this dilemma. He felt that God was trying to tell him something, but what could the message be?

It took George a little time before he was able to understand God's message. The Divine being wanted George to move onto another path of service. George listened to the inner voice that he knew was his link with the Divine and, before long, George knew what he had to do. He entered medicine. He would serve in a different manner and follow what he believed to be God's plan for him.

George graduated with honors in medicine from the University of Manitoba in 1916. He was second in standing in his class. One year later, he accepted a six month position as medical superintendent of a tuberculosis treatment center. He retained that position and battled against the dreaded T.B. which ravaged the plains Indians and the whites, alike.

As the years passed, and his agenda became busier, he did not attend church. However, he possessed a clear "Image" of his God. This "Image" had allowed George to hear his calling of service at an early age. It had helped him to awaken to that calling and undertake to respond through aiding his family, entering the ministry, then becoming a medical doctor.

He knew that personal experience of God was the gift of faith and devotion. He often experienced God as he helped the sick back to health or helped the grievously ill in their process of dying. The God he felt was the same.

George had served God in fulfilling the greatest of all commandments, to love God and his fellow man.

George once wrote about his image of God as a God of character and worth. He felt that God was,

> Wise, understanding, honest, and just
> A respected creator and co-ordinator
> A source of Peace
> A source of Power
> The Spirit that pervaded the Universe
> A source of the spirit breathed into man as the breath of life and
>     limited divinity

George's spiritual emergence was a lifelong commitment to the calling he heard as a boy.

## The Story of Alfred

In the year 1941, a large, rotund, and slightly flat-footed 30 year old man stood in the recruitment line. As he observed the young, fit men around him who were also waiting to enlist, he shook his head. It was impossible to think that the army would accept him. He was too old, too flabby, certainly not capable of bearing arms in the growing conflaguration in Europe or in the Pacific. As he questioned himself he then reflected on his dream of two nights previous.

A wonderful Divine being had told Alfred that he was to enlist in the army. The 'voice' told him that God needed him to help save men caught in despair.

Alfred winced as he thought about this dream. Maybe he had imagined the angel? Alfred caught himself. God had talked to him through a vision. The feeling of peace and acceptance that he felt was no illusion. He would see what would happen.

Alfred found himself before the recruitment officer. They smiled at each other and then began their dialogue. The officer wanted to know Alfred's vital statistics and reasons for enlisting. He also asked about Alfred's past history and talents.

Alfred's life had been unexciting. He had never married, but had lived and supported his widowed mother through the depression years. His great love was music and mimicking. In his younger years, Alfred hoped to study music and make that his career. However, life had played strange tricks and Alfred had found himself working as an orderly .

He was known as the 'Al Jolson' of the wards for he would break into song as he pushed carts down the long infirmary halls. He often sang to the ill children as he mimicked and pranced in rhythm to his strong, able voice. He arranged musicals for the hospital patients and found himself in charge of recreation. Everyone loved Alfred and he loved them.

Life had indeed been strange. Alfred no longer questioned his pathway for he had been well schooled by his mother. 'God always has a plan', she had told him, but the trick was in recognizing it.

The recruitment officer told Alfred that it was doubtful that the army would accept him. As he uttered these words, a commanding officer appeared from the backroom and looked at Alfred's application. The commander asked Alfred to accompany him. Within minutes, Alfred had been inducted into the army. Everyone, except Albert, was amazed.

Two years passed. Alfred had been posted as a medical assistant in the Pacific. He watched as young men, on both sides, fought and killed one another. He worked to heal those who were wounded and scarred. He kept singing. The men loved this strange man who was full of jokes, stories, and music. He helped them remember the good times...the times of peace.

There was no time to react. The enemy swooped down and captured the little island where Alfred was stationed. He found himself as a prisoner of war. The first night in this captive state, he once again experienced a vision as he slept. The Divine being reappeared to him and told him that God needed him more than ever and that Alfred would live throught the war.

Alfred, then, began to understand God's plan more clearly. He was the singing orderly. He was to heal men's bodies and to lift their spirits through song. He was to be a light in the midst of the darkness.

The next three years passed slowly. There was never sufficient food or heat, never enough medical supplies, never enough news about the war. Alfred kept singing while he attended to the sick and dying men of the prisoner camp. He thought that he, too, would perish. His weight fell to 75 pounds and, at times, he thought he would go mad with the experience of continued inhumanity.

But Alfred never gave up. He kept singing. The men loved him and his captors respected him.

Liberation came finally. Alfred was able to walk out of the prisoner camp. He was exhausted and ill, but he had carried out God's plan and felt he had been God's instrument.

Eventually, Alfred returned to his hospital wards. The world was at peace. Alfred's voice was deeper and richer as he sang his 'ditties' and pranced in rhythm down the infirmary halls.

## The Story of Evelyn

In the year 1966, a fifty year old woman stood in the rural church beside three coffins. She looked at the caskets which held the remains of her family members. Two of her four children and her father had been killed in an automobile accident. In seconds, her family had been destroyed, her children gone.

The woman trembled as she looked at the cross at the front of the church. She had always believed in God and had been an active participant in her church. She had extended her 'helping hand' to neighbors and friends, alike. She had lived a devoted life to God, others, and herself. Now, God had taken three of the people who she loved the most. She leaned on the arm of her ill husband. How could God have allowed this? Did He really need her children and father more than she? She studied the cross as the minister read from the Bible. The words tumbled together. Evelyn could hear nothing except the sounds of crying mourners.

Evelyn wanted to blame her 80 year old father for his lack of driving attentiveness. It had been he who had errored on the highway and had caused the accident. She thought of her father. He had adopted her in her infancy. His love and commitment to her throughout her entire life had stabilized Evelyn. He had been a minister and had taught her to love God before all others. How could she now blame her father, who had given her so much and had helped her formulate her philosophy of life? There was no one to blame except God, and Evelyn didn't feel wise enough to do that. God must have a reason for calling her family members home.

After the funeral service, Evelyn moved amongst the people who had come to show their respects. There were children, classmates, and friends of her deceased children, and adults, and seniors, and friends of her parents. The church hall overflowed with mourners who were barely able to speak, they seemed so stunned with grief. Evelyn began to talk with individuals in whispered tones. She heard the same question uttered by many during that long day. How could God allow this to happen? Always, her response was the same. It was impossible to know and understand God's plan. But

God must have loved them greatly and wanted them to return home.

As Evelyn repeated this throughout the day, she began to feel the words. She had prayed for understanding, but was unsure as to how she would ever gain acceptance of God's plan. However, her defence of God began to calm her. The words she spoke began to move through her heart and she felt a slight peace and calmness. The more she spoke the words of understanding, the greater was her own. As she left the church hall and returned home with her fragmented family, she felt a glimpse of awareness.

Fifteen years later, Evelyn was called by the lay council of the same Church. They explained that the minister had retired and no replacement could be found. They had deliberated amongst themselves and unanimously decided to offer the position to Evelyn.

She had shown outstanding courage in the face of enormous personal tests. Her love and devotion to God was a testament of her faith. No one was more fit than she to speak about relationship with the Creator. As they explained their reasons for choosing her, Evelyn felt true humility. She was just a simple woman who had survived tremendous tests. It was true that her love of God was stronger and that she depended on Him to help her through her day. After a great deal of contemplation, Evelyn decided to minister to her community until a suitable replacement could be found.

Six months later, her phone rang in the middle of the night. The voice on the end of the phone cried that a school bus filled with teens had been hit by a semi-trailer. Could she come and help with the overwrought parents? As she hurried out of bed, she sank to her knees.

God's plan encircled her and her heart felt true peace.

# EPILOGUE

## "PREPARERS of the WAY"

This time of transition in which we live is a time of tremendous personal internal and material external changes that are impacting all levels of our earthly existence. Each of us will be tested, challenged, and provided the opportunity to see ourselves in different ways.

This internal revolution which occurs as a result of our pursuit of the truth of the Divine can be filled with confusion, dismay, and a true sense of exhaustion or soul fatigue.

Our attempt to help enlighten and lighten the weight that the children who seek the light carry is the formation of an international and open-membership NETWORK. We know the uniqueness of the path that each individual walks for we have walked this path ourselves. We know the loneliness and the misunderstanding that can be caused by others in our life, for we've felt them ourselves. We know the sense of hopelessness and the growing desire to go home that is born of our earthly limitation and confinement, for we've desired that ourselves.

Our contribution and the purpose that stands behind the network is to help to inform, awaken, and support the expression of the light and love of the Divine that can be found within.

The sharing of information will be in a variety of forms, all working to bring a greater awareness of the impacts that the planetary shift in consciousness will have on our earthly lives. This knowledge may aid in awakening us to the active presence of the Divine both internally and externally. Once we grow in awareness and become more firm in our understanding, we can aid each other to gather and support the expression of our soul's purpose in the earth.

Initially, the Preparers of the Way will be a simple network that seeks to gather those who resonate to the spirit of truth seeking and light-seeing that resides within its very name. A newsletter will be published quarterly that will contain advice and counsel on the purpose and the meaning that underlies the "events" that are currently transforming the planet. The advice and counsel will be sourced from the etheric or the heavenly realms, and will serve to give a wholistic perspective on the shift.

In time, the Preparers of the Way will evolve into different forms and expressions as will be needed and appropriate for these rapidly changing times. But for now it will remain a simple network that will offer books, tapes, lectures, and seminars.

All who feel called to participate are welcome, either to help creatively express their talents and abilities through the framework of the purposes and principles embodied in this book, or to receive sustenance from the information that is shared and evolves from this network.

In each age and cycle of learning for mankind, there were those who were sent to give a new understanding and a new application of the one truth. How this spirit of truth came is first to the individual who had prepared the way in themselves to receive it. Once claimed, there would grow the desire to be of service and to help prepare the way in others.

Each relationship that is formed gives an opportunity for mutual learning and mutual healing. We hope and pray that you will find the peace and stability that your heart yearns for when you enter into an intimate relationship with the Divine.

For it is in that great relationship that you will find that all your questions will be answered, all your desires will be fulfilled, and the path that you need to walk will be illuminated.

This book is a story that never ends, for the story of man's growth and ascent continues so long as there is one soul who has not awakened to his Divine heritage. Life is a continuum and each event builds on the last and weaves itself into the tapestry that is the soul of man.

We began this work in peace and in love and we leave this work the same as it began...in PEACE and in LOVE.

*Preparers of the Way*
*P.O. BOX 22204 - Bankers Hall*
*Calgary, Alberta, CANADA T2P-4J5*

# ABOUT THE AUTHORS

The authors have experienced every facet of preparation, awakening, and cleansing described within this book. Each was awakened by a calling which resulted in a haunting and growing desire for truth and relationship with the Divine. Their paths, although very different, were similar in that each was motivated to prepare the way, first in themselves, and then in others.

**RICK HATALA** is a professional engineer who, when faced with a career decision, sought for a truer understanding of his life's mission. He began with the study of comparative religions and the work of Edgar Cayce and then furthered his exploration by examining philosophy, psychology, parapsychology, and wholistic healing. Over the past seven years, while pursuing his engineering vocation, he has taught seminars, workshops, and written articles on the many facets of spirituality.

**SHANNON SAMBELLS** first awakened to her calling through a Divine vision received during a meditation nearly ten years ago. This caused her to search for inner attunement with her Image of God. She worked and communed with those in the etheric, first for herself, and then for others worldwide, through her spiritually channeled readings. She has conducted lectures, workshops, and seminars on the relationship between psychic and spiritual development. She is the mother of three and presently resides in Canada.

The authors feel that The Calling of the Children of the Light is a fulfillment of their souls' mission which is to help to awaken others to a personal and intimate relationship with the Divine.